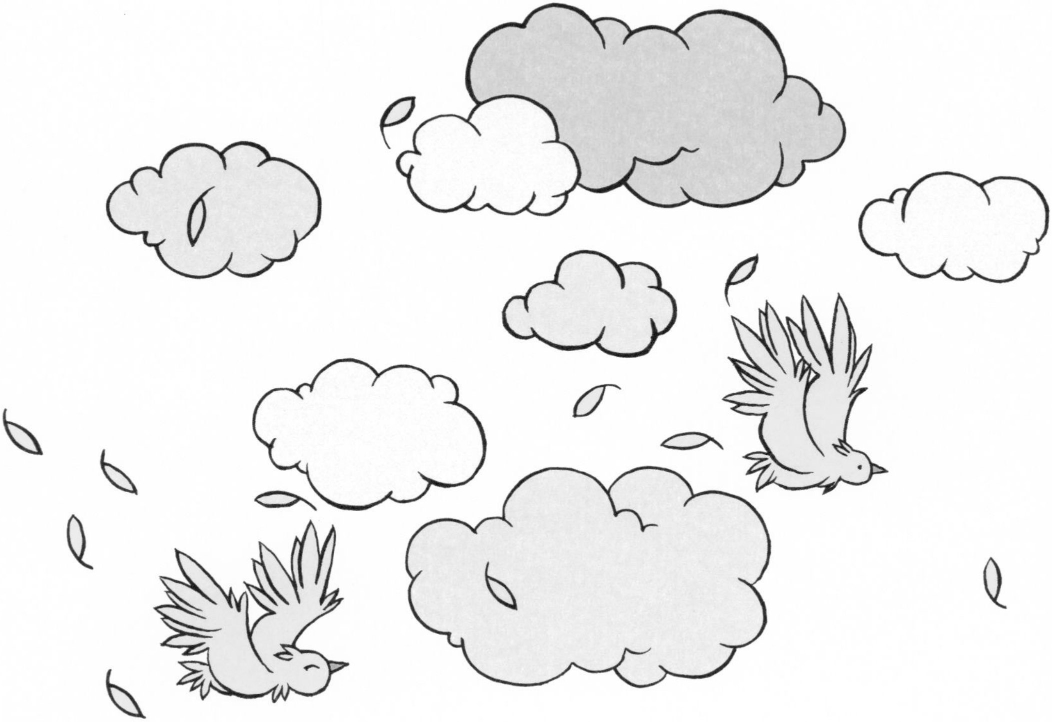

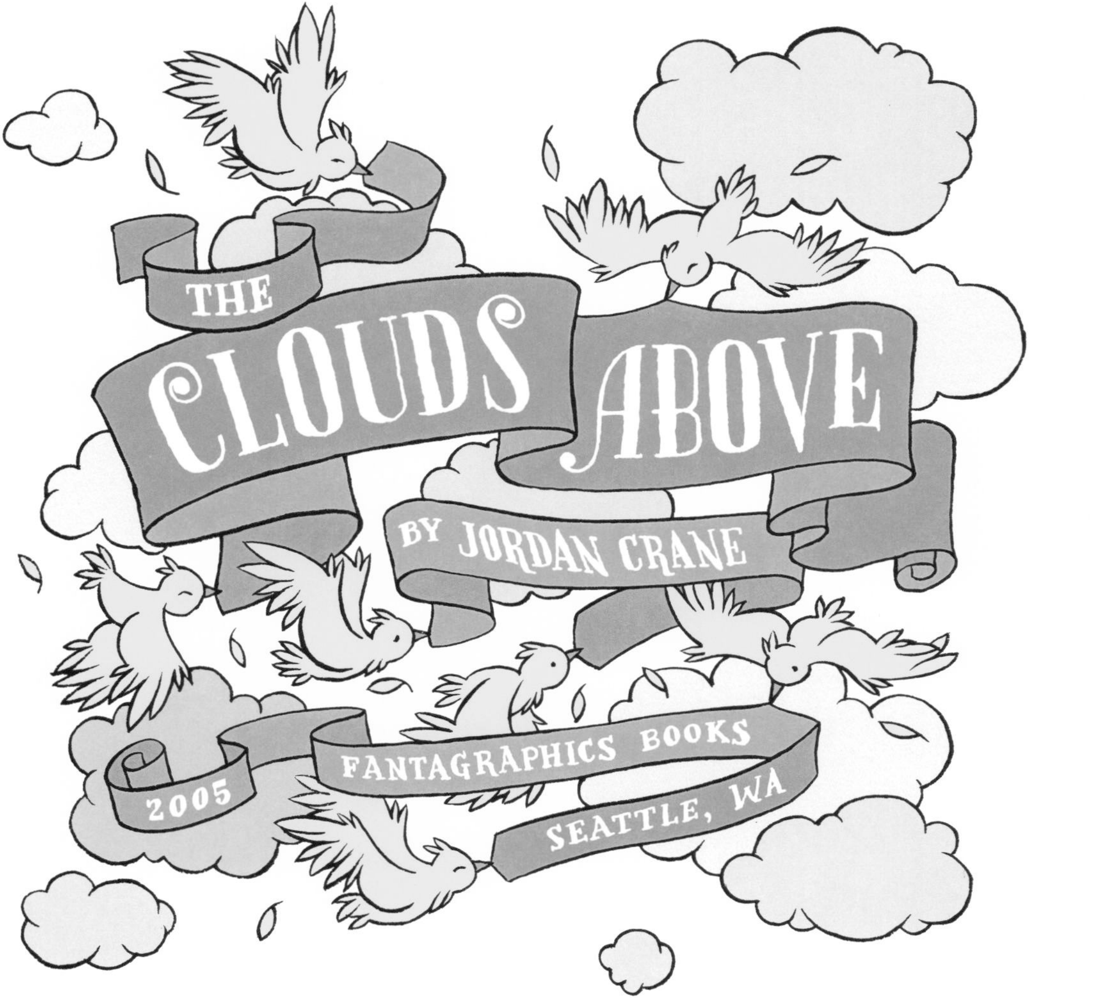
THE
CLOUDS ABOVE
BY JORDAN CRANE
2005
FANTAGRAPHICS BOOKS
SEATTLE, WA

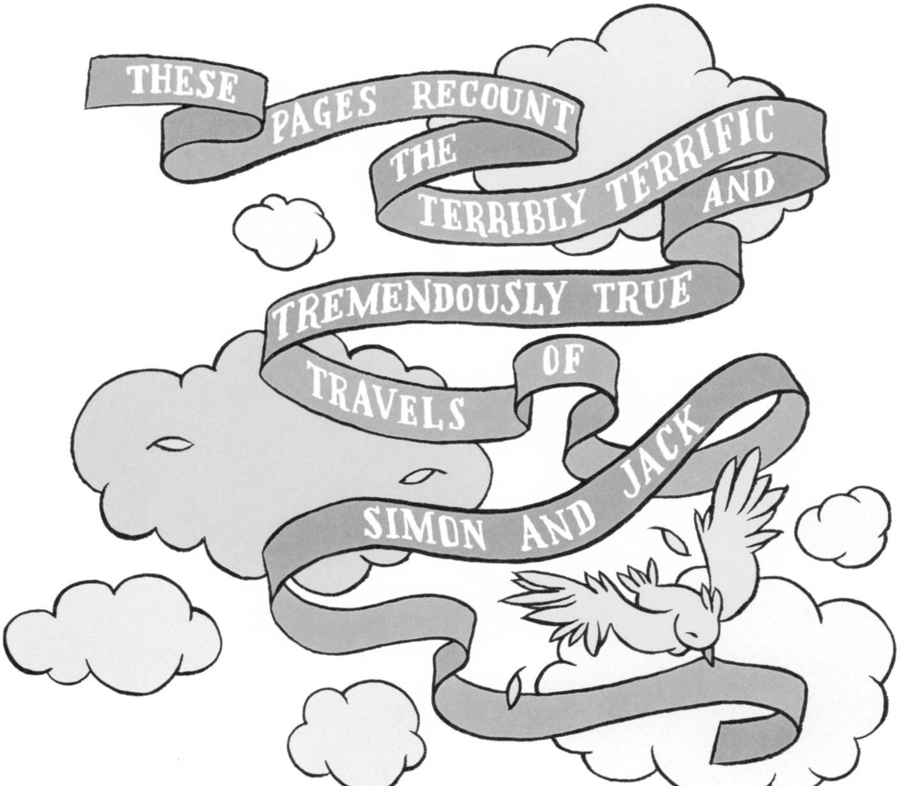
THESE PAGES RECOUNT THE TERRIBLY TERRIFIC AND TREMENDOUSLY TRUE TRAVELS OF SIMON AND JACK

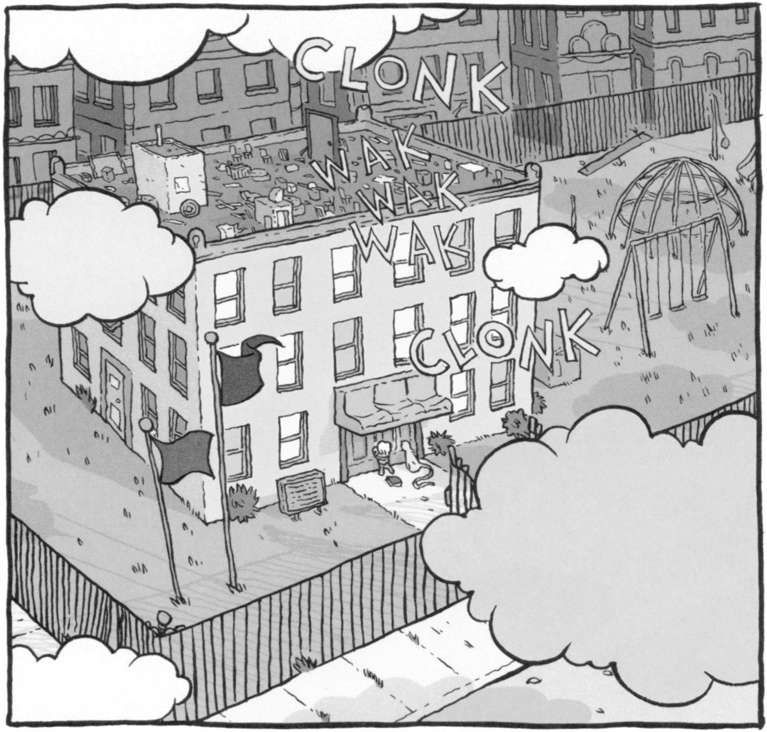

CLONK
WAK
WAK
WAK
CLONK

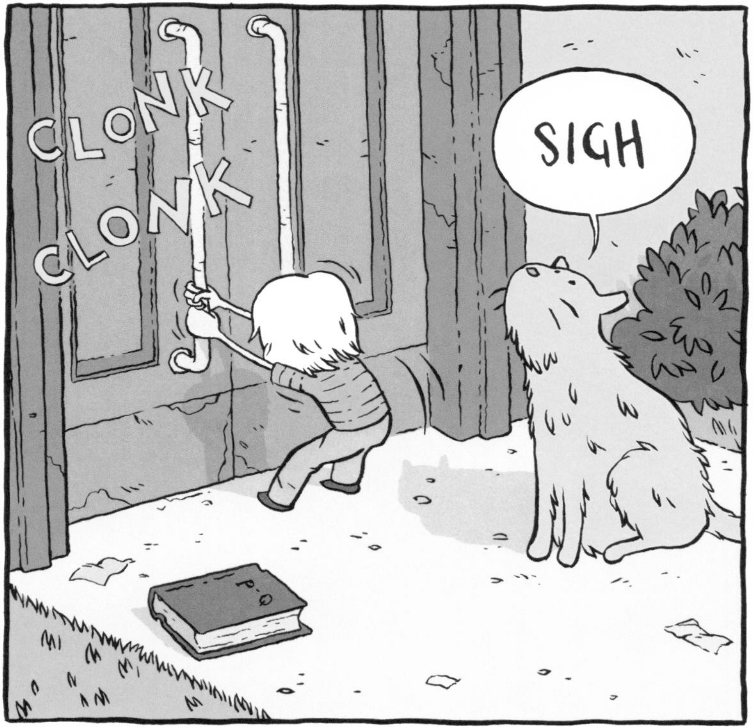
CLONK
CLONK
SIGH
P.Q

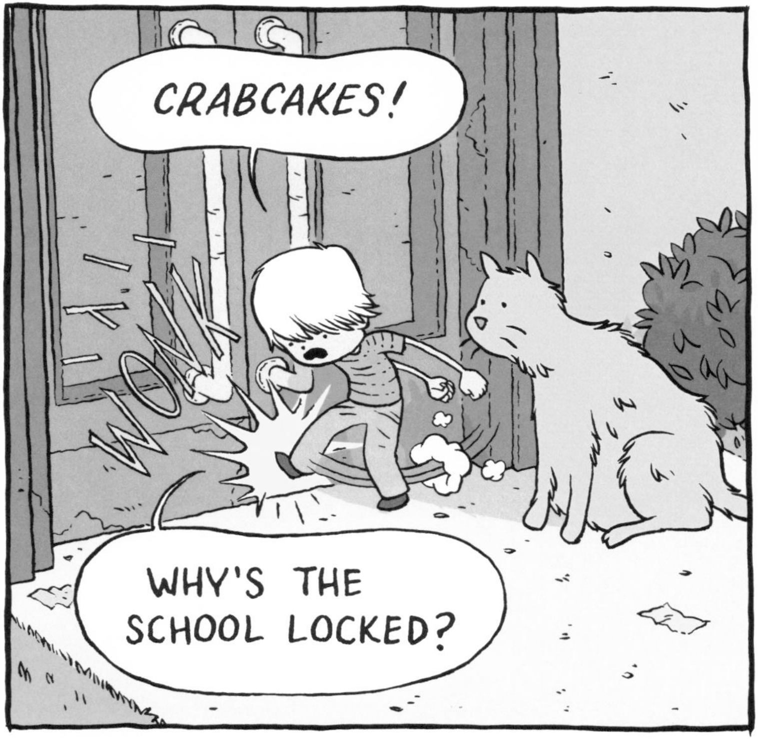
CRABCAKES!
WONK
WHY'S THE SCHOOL LOCKED?

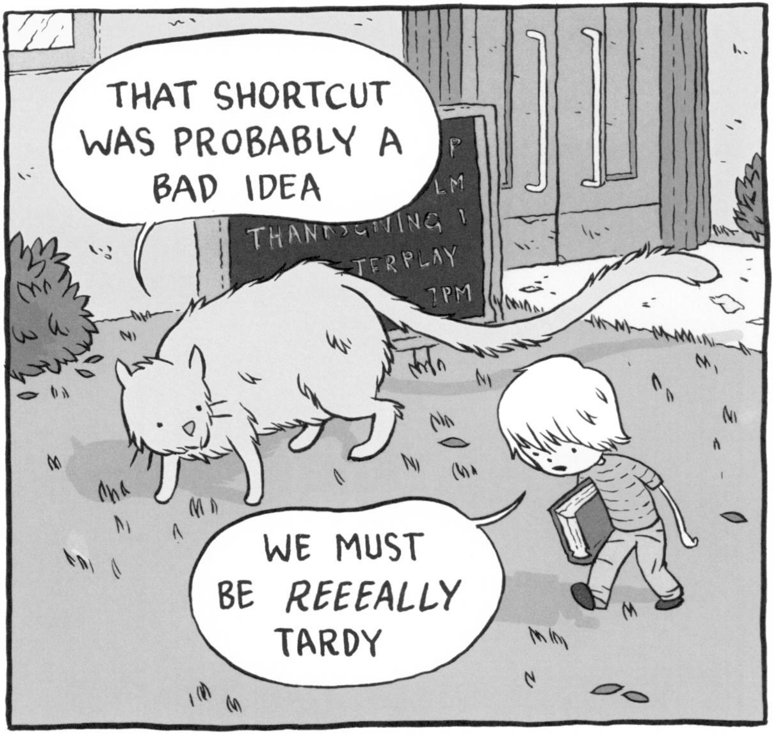
THAT SHORTCUT WAS PROBABLY A BAD IDEA
WE MUST BE *REEEALLY* TARDY

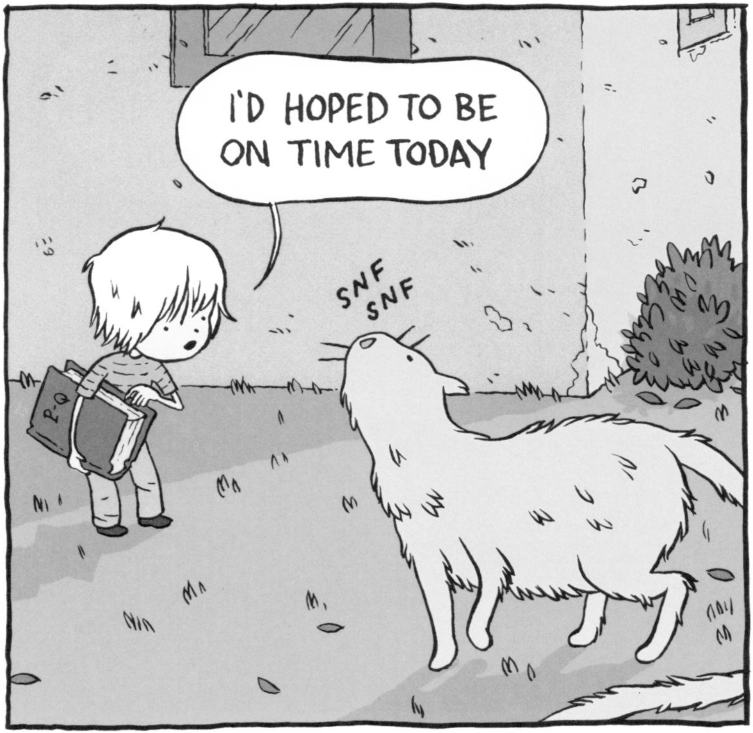
I'D HOPED TO BE ON TIME TODAY
SNF SNF
P-Q

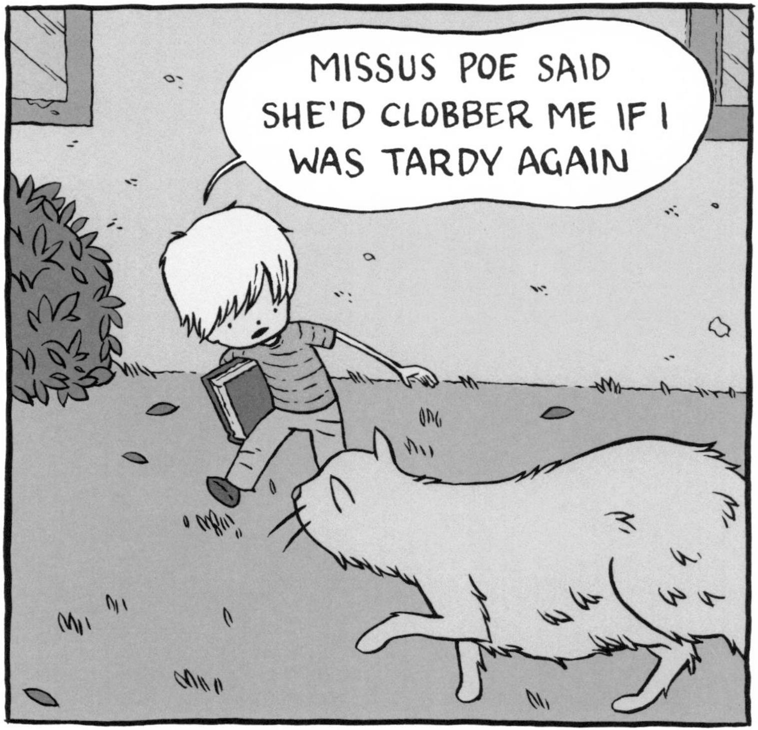
MISSUS POE SAID SHE'D CLOBBER ME IF I WAS TARDY AGAIN

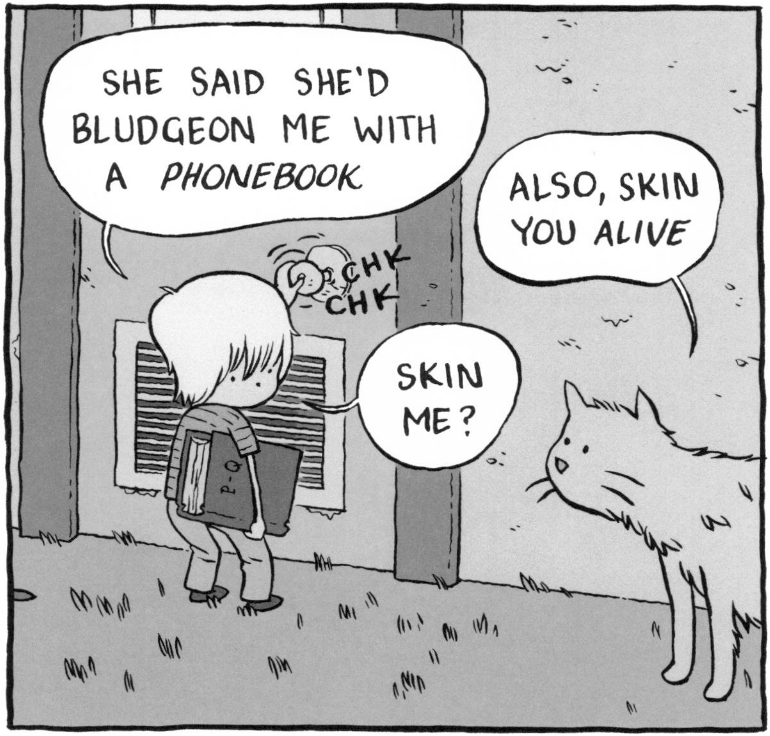
SHE SAID SHE'D BLUDGEON ME WITH A *PHONEBOOK*
CHK CHK
SKIN ME?
ALSO, SKIN YOU *ALIVE*
P-Q

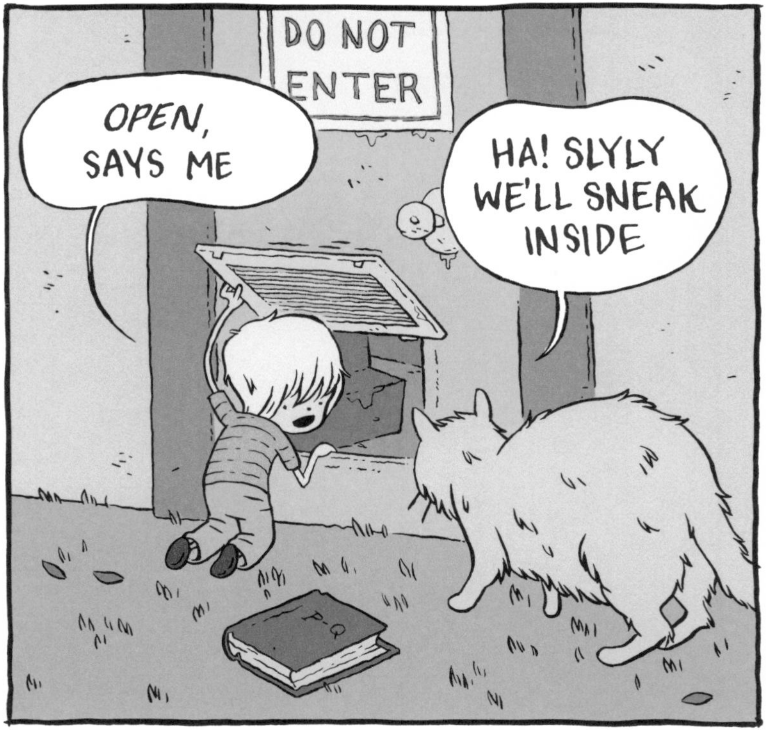
DO NOT ENTER
OPEN, SAYS ME
HA! SLYLY WE'LL SNEAK INSIDE
P-Q

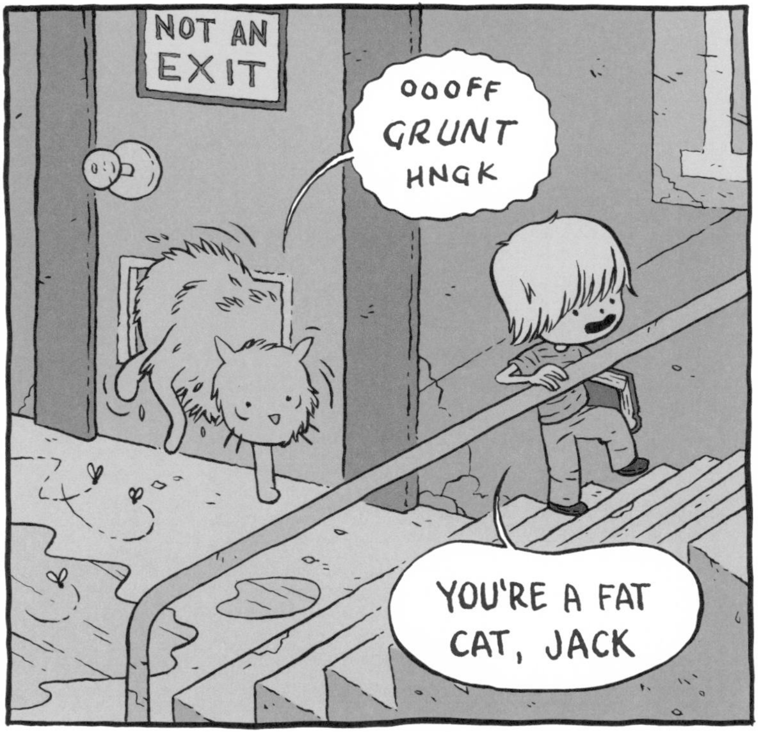
NOT AN EXIT
OOOFF GRUNT HNGK
YOU'RE A FAT CAT, JACK

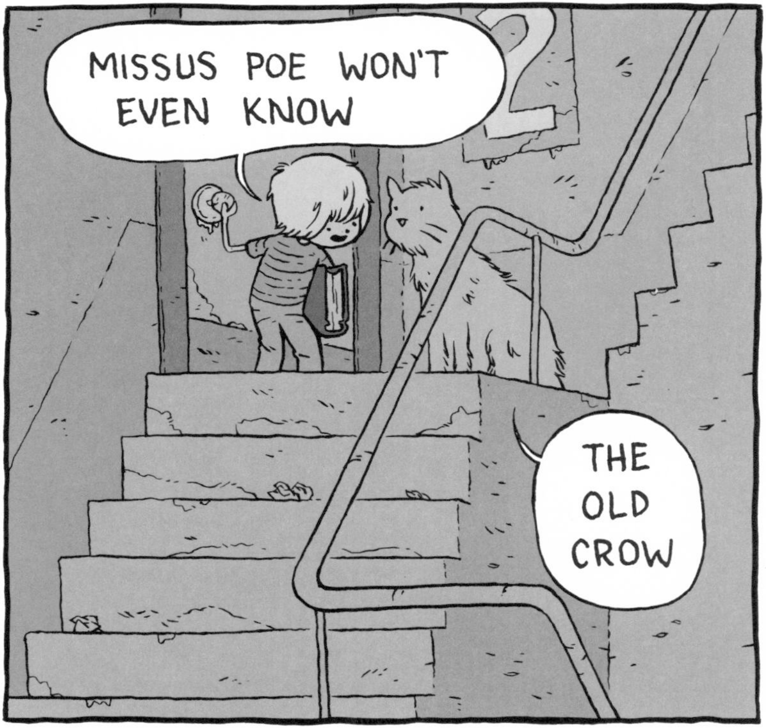
MISSUS POE WON'T EVEN KNOW
THE OLD CROW

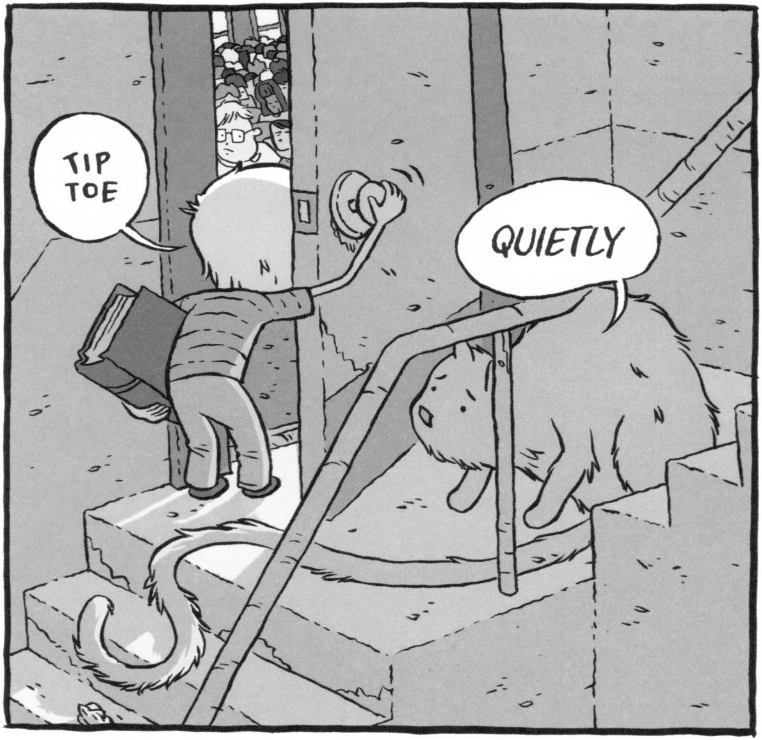
TIP TOE
QUIETLY

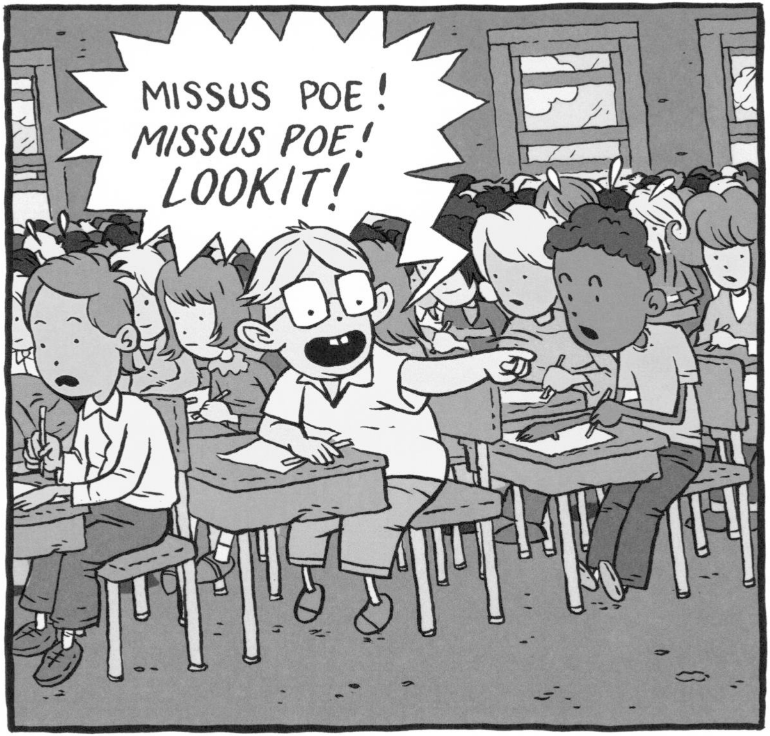
MISSUS POE! MISSUS POE! LOOKIT!

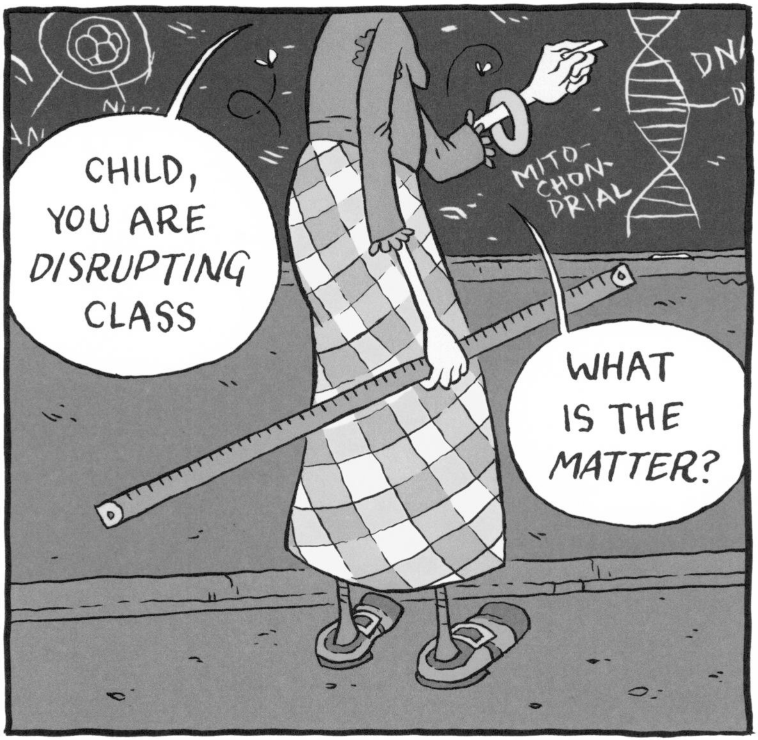
MITO-
CHON-
DRIAL
DNA
CHILD, YOU ARE *DISRUPTING* CLASS
WHAT IS THE *MATTER?*

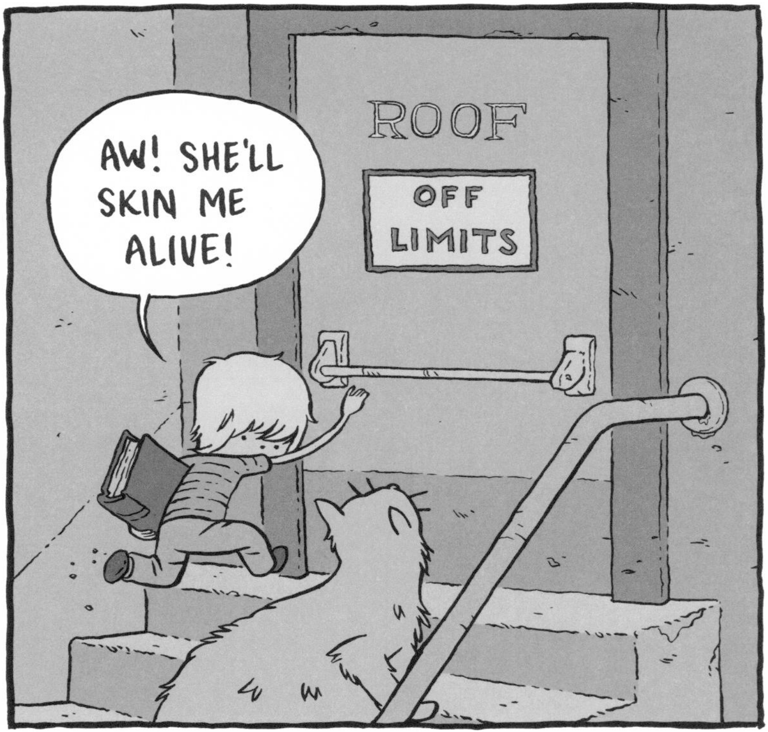
ROOF
OFF LIMITS
AW! SHE'LL SKIN ME ALIVE!

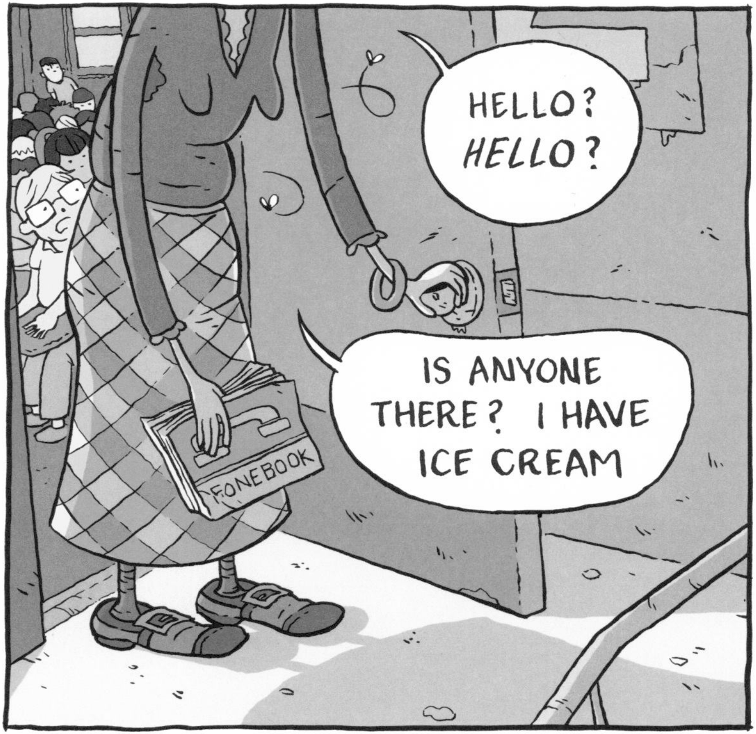

HELLO? HELLO?
IS ANYONE THERE? I HAVE ICE CREAM
FONEBOOK

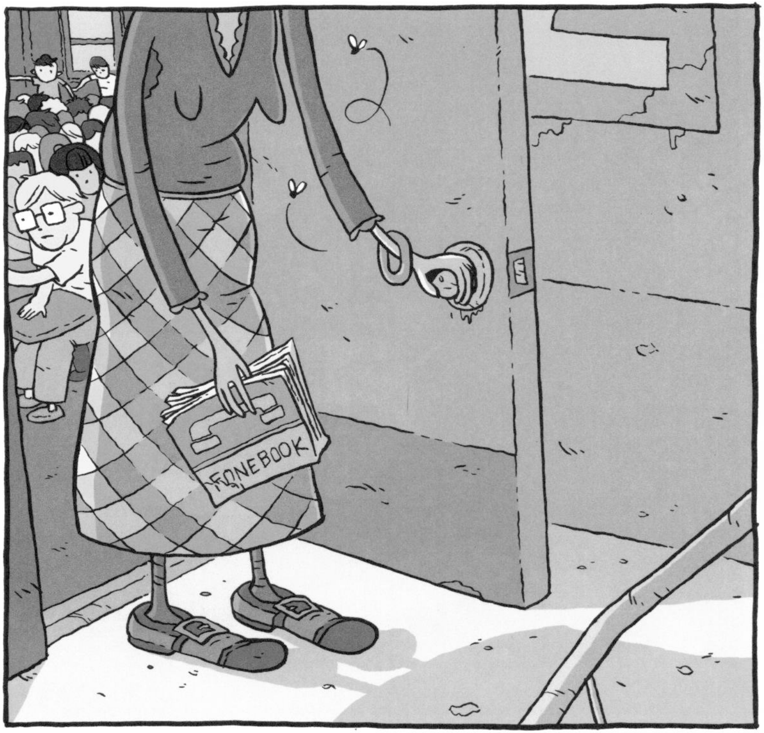
FONEBOOK

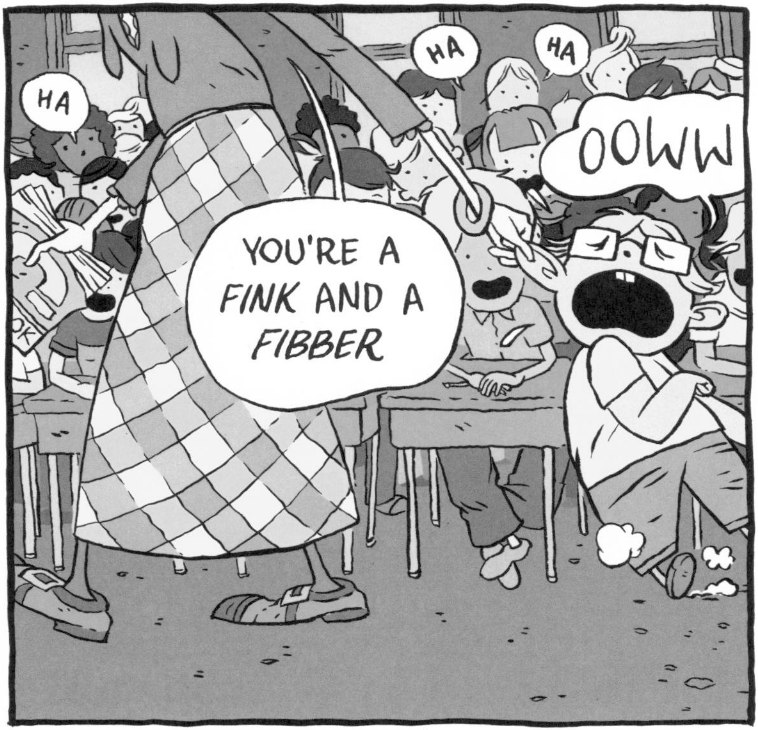
HA
HA
HA
OOWW
YOU'RE A FINK AND A FIBBER

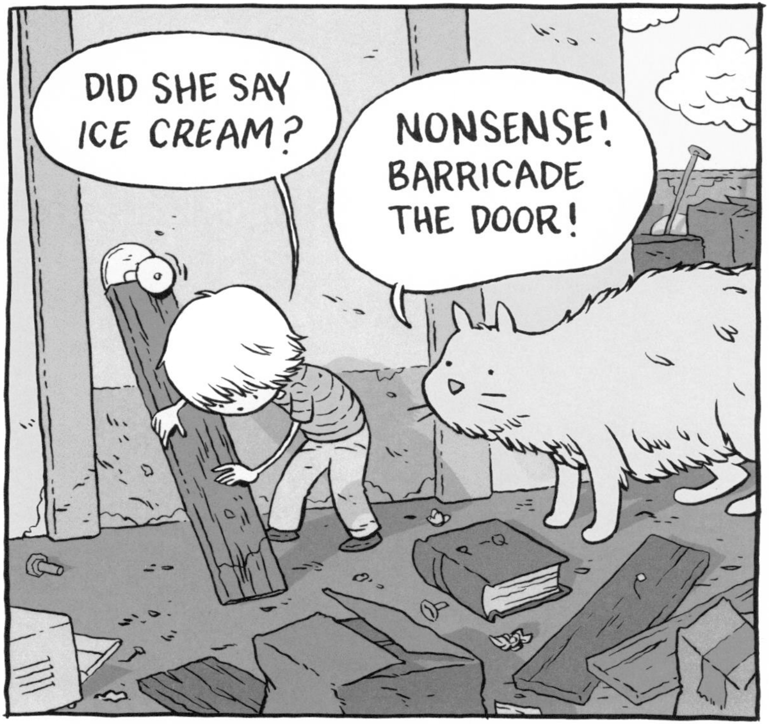
DID SHE SAY ICE CREAM?
NONSENSE! BARRICADE THE DOOR!

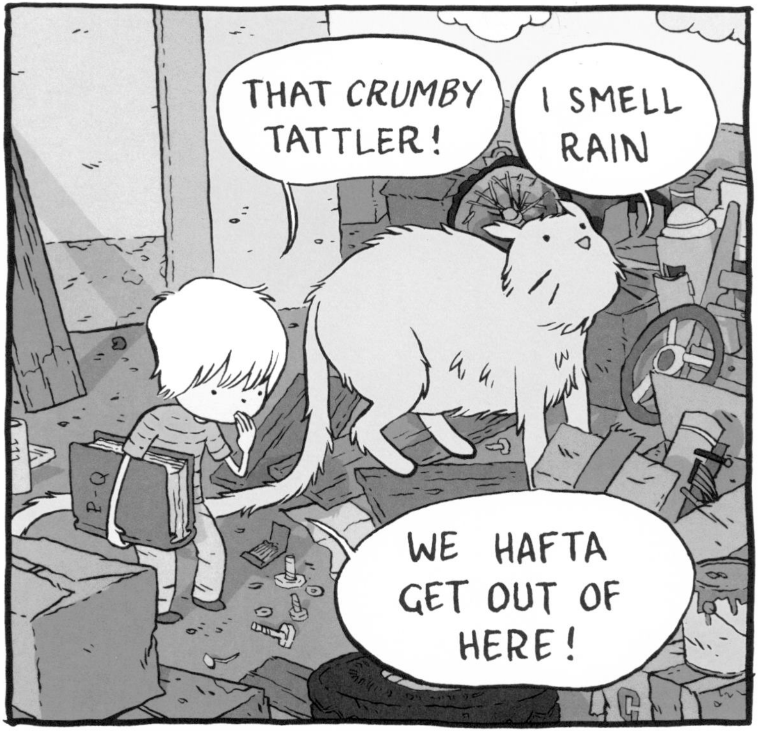
THAT CRUMBY TATTLER!
I SMELL RAIN
WE HAFTA GET OUT OF HERE!

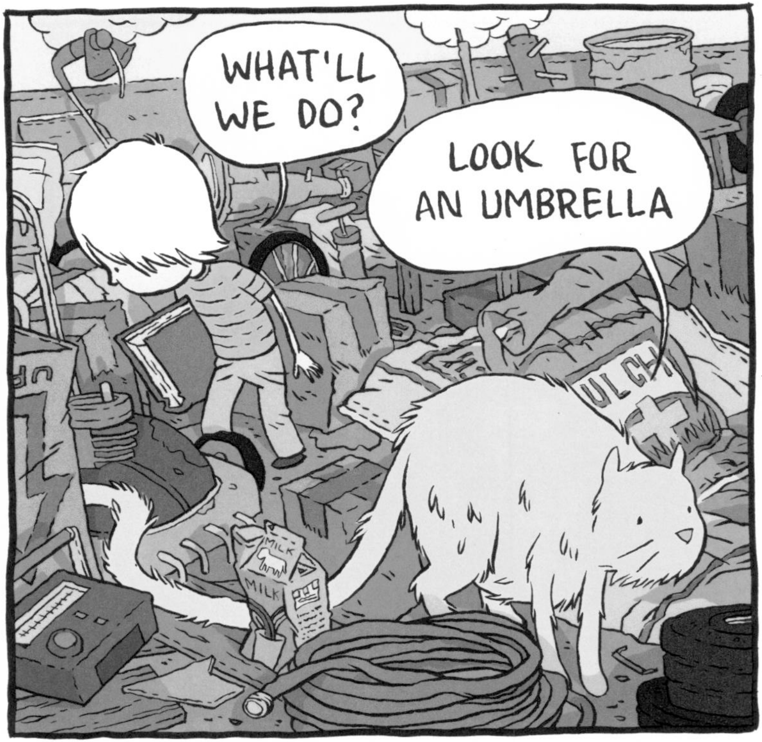
WHAT'LL WE DO?
LOOK FOR AN UMBRELLA
MILK
MILK
UP

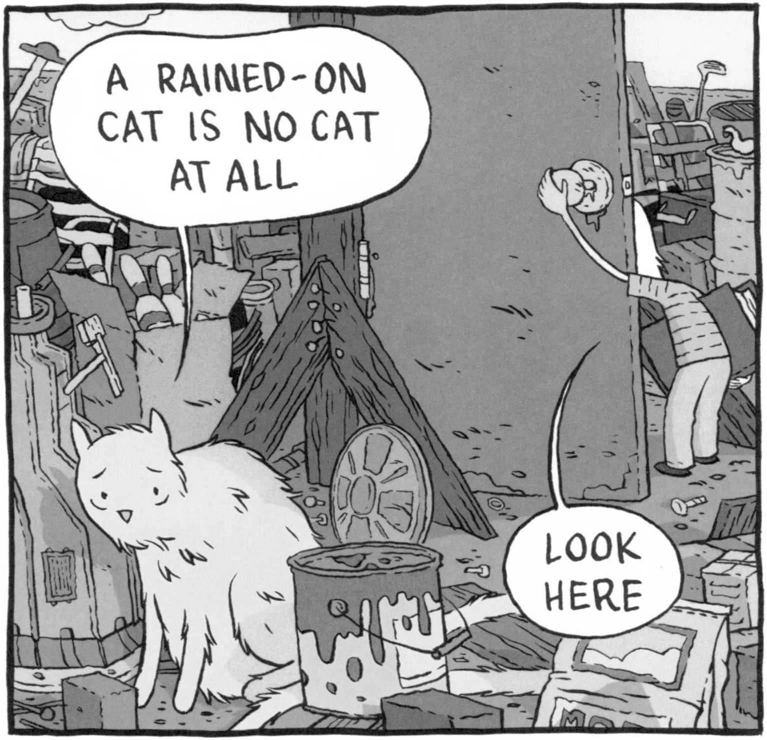
A RAINED-ON CAT IS NO CAT AT ALL
LOOK HERE

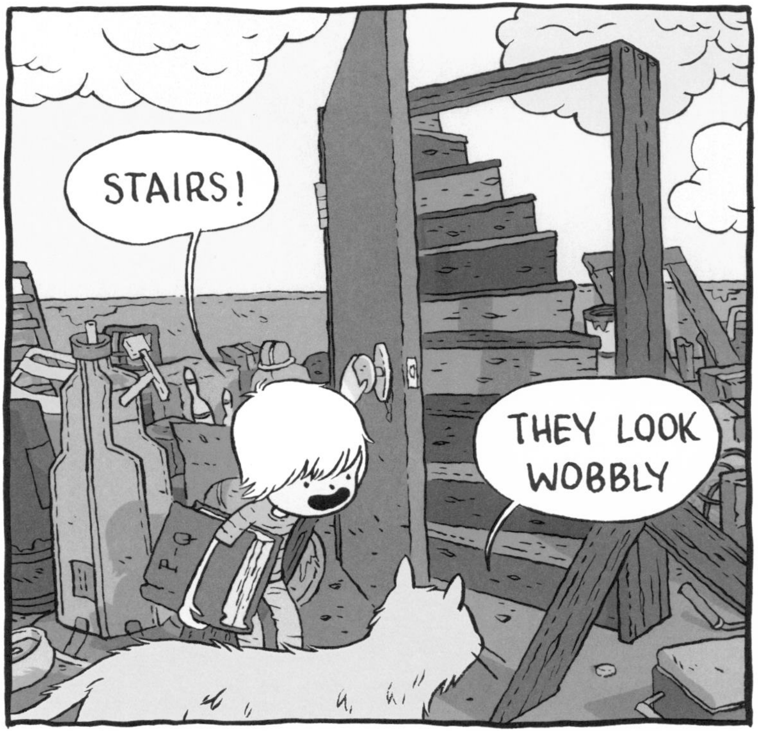
STAIRS!
THEY LOOK WOBBLY

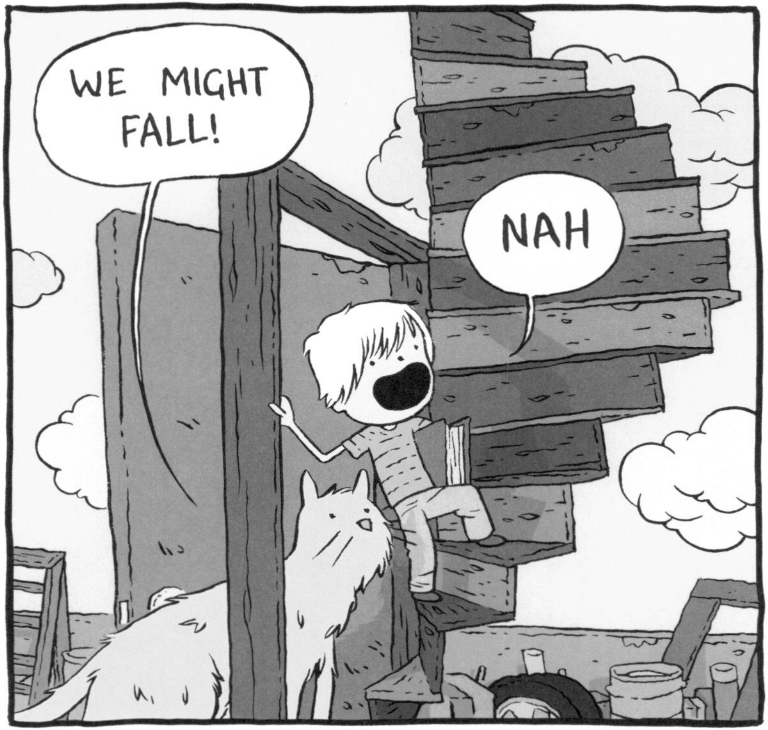
WE MIGHT FALL!
NAH

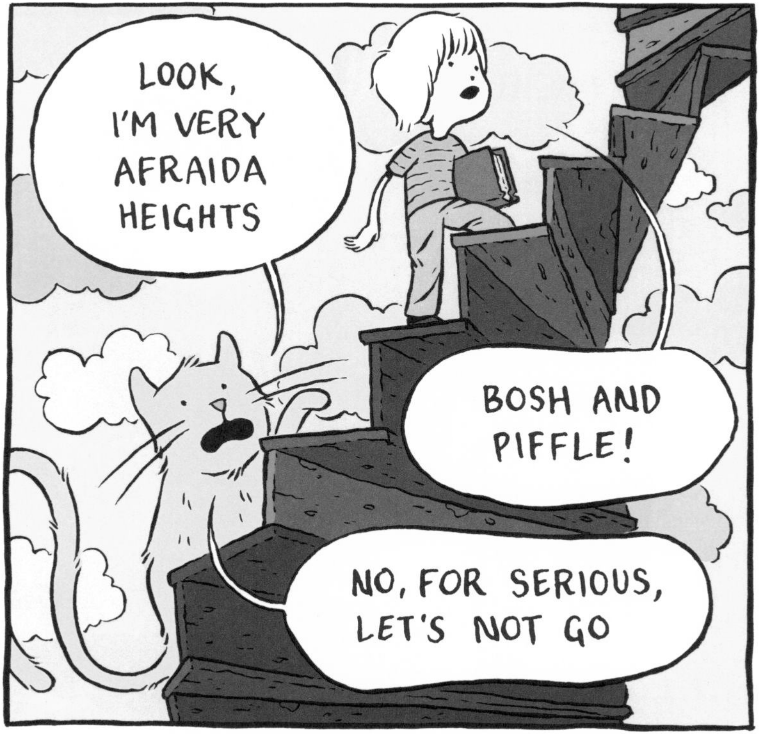
LOOK, I'M VERY AFRAIDA HEIGHTS
BOSH AND PIFFLE!
NO, FOR SERIOUS, LET'S NOT GO

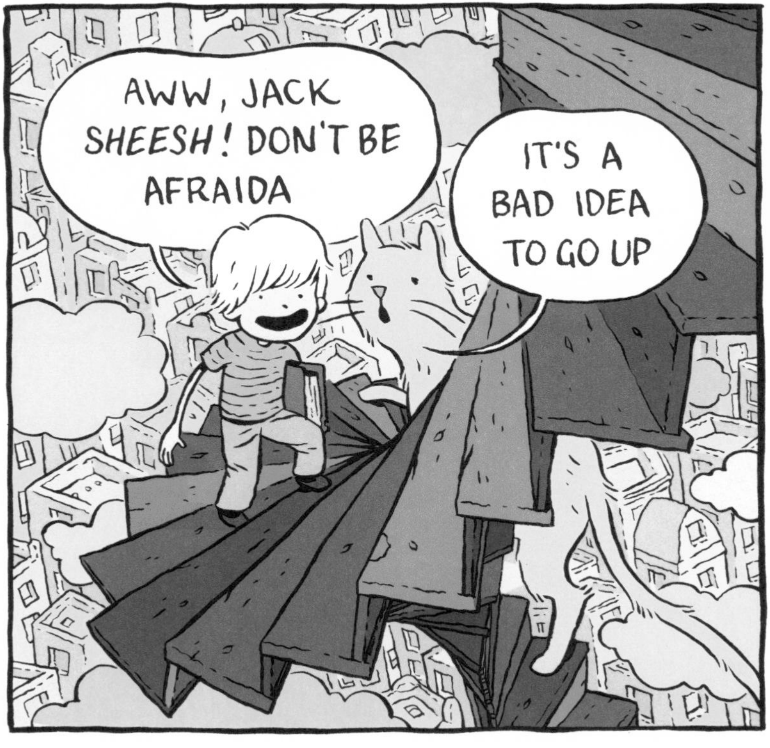
AWW, JACK SHEESH! DON'T BE AFRAIDA
IT'S A BAD IDEA TO GO UP

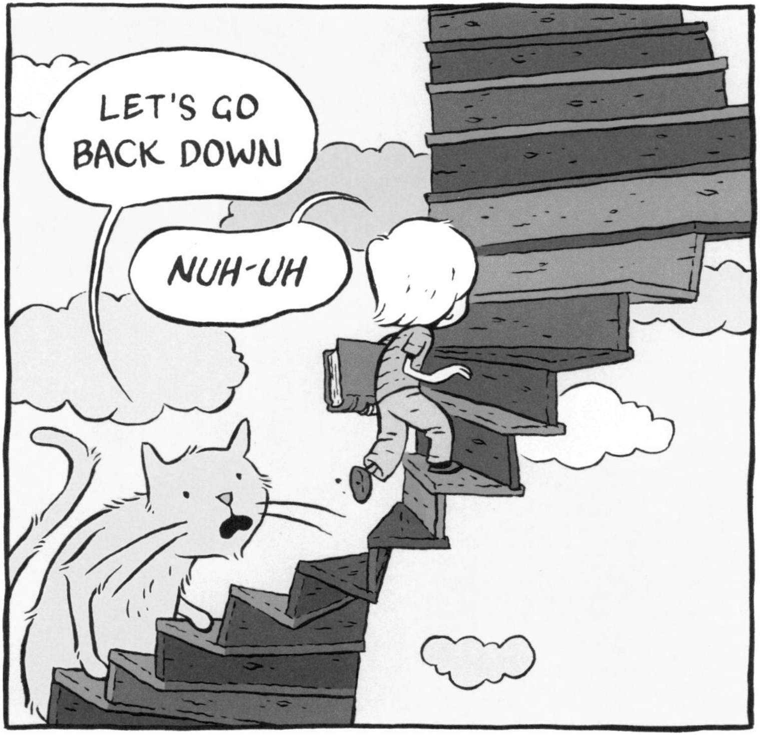
LET'S GO BACK DOWN
NUH-UH

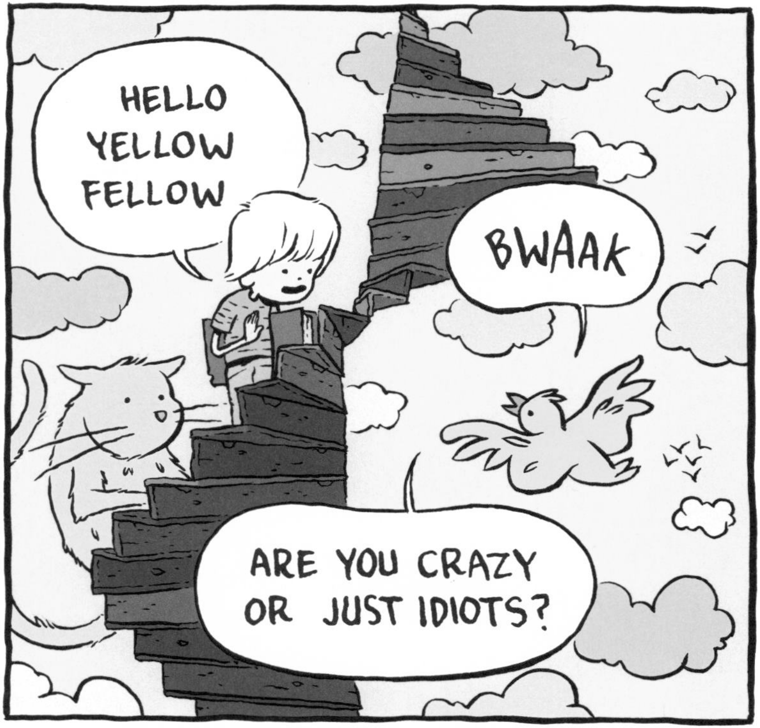
HELLO YELLOW FELLOW
BWAAK
ARE YOU CRAZY OR JUST IDIOTS?

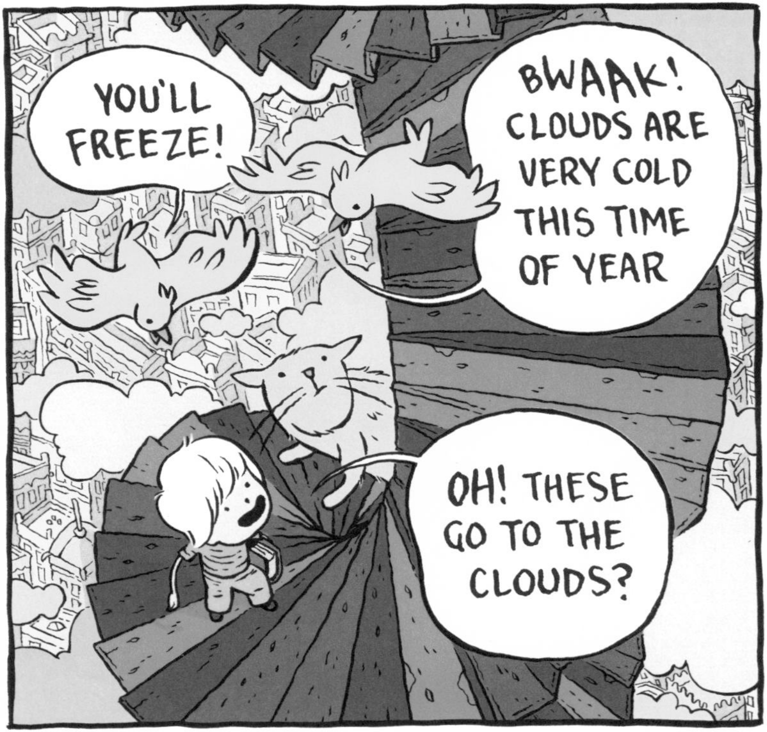
YOU'LL FREEZE!
BWAAK! CLOUDS ARE VERY COLD THIS TIME OF YEAR
OH! THESE GO TO THE CLOUDS?

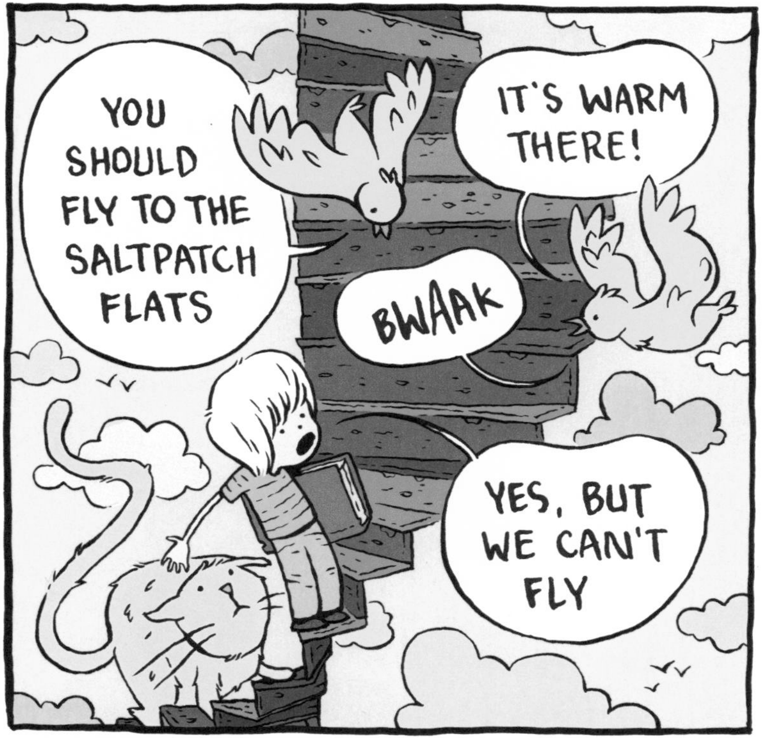
YOU SHOULD FLY TO THE SALTPATCH FLATS
IT'S WARM THERE!
BWAAK
YES, BUT WE CAN'T FLY

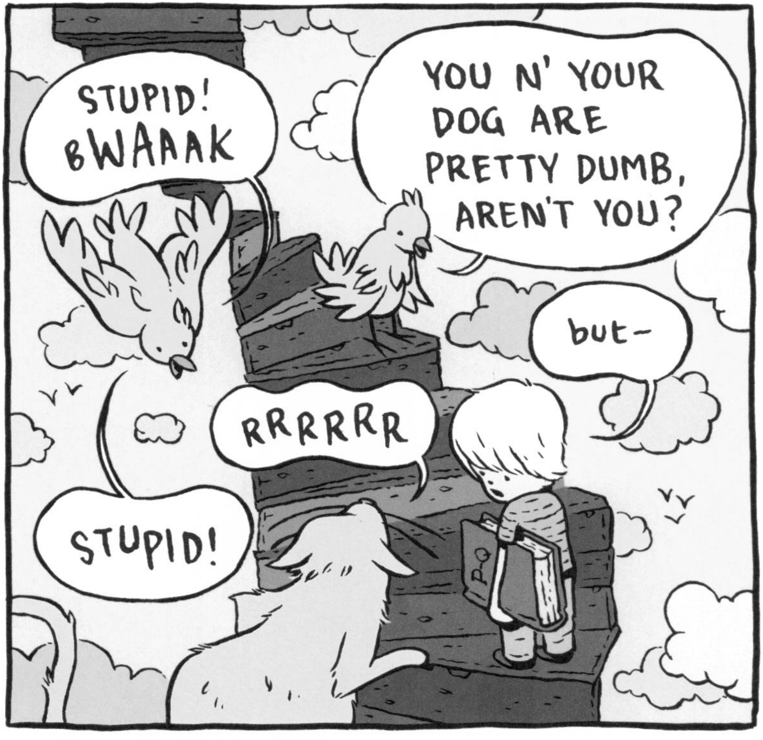
STUPID! BWAAAK
YOU N' YOUR DOG ARE PRETTY DUMB, AREN'T YOU?
but-
RRRRRRR
STUPID!

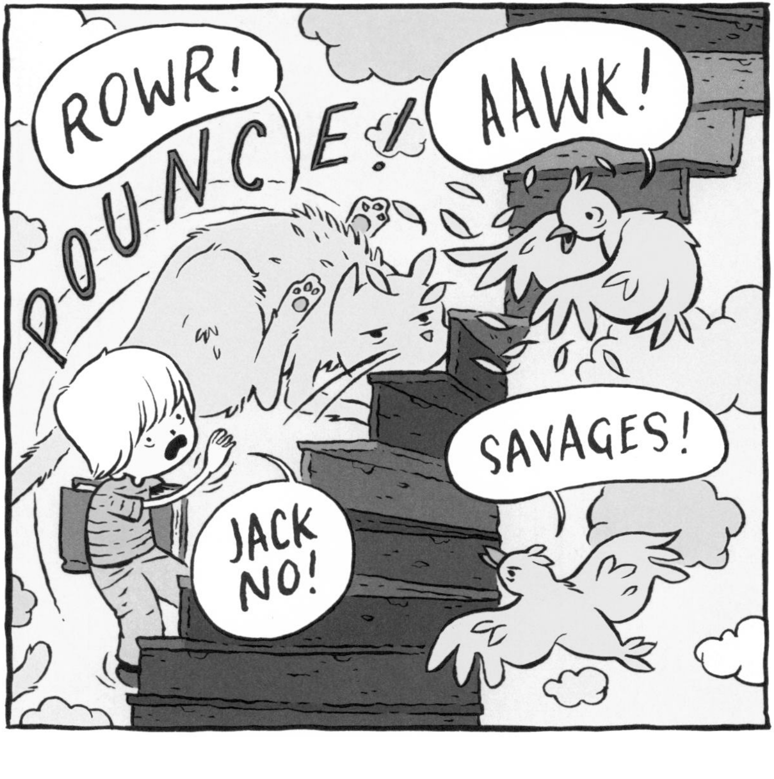
ROWR!
POUNCE!
AAWK!
SAVAGES!
JACK NO!

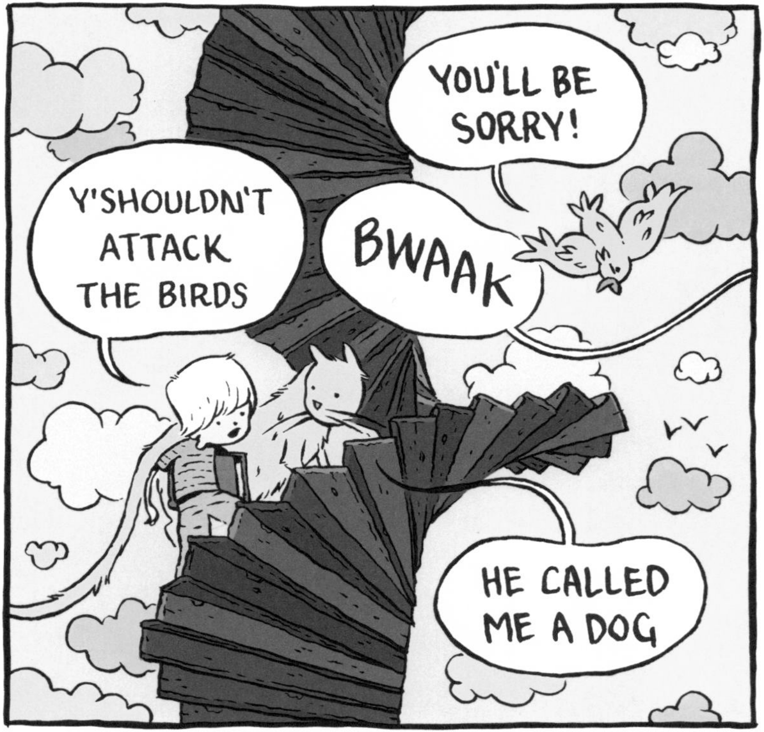
Y'SHOULDN'T ATTACK THE BIRDS
YOU'LL BE SORRY!
BWAAK
HE CALLED ME A DOG

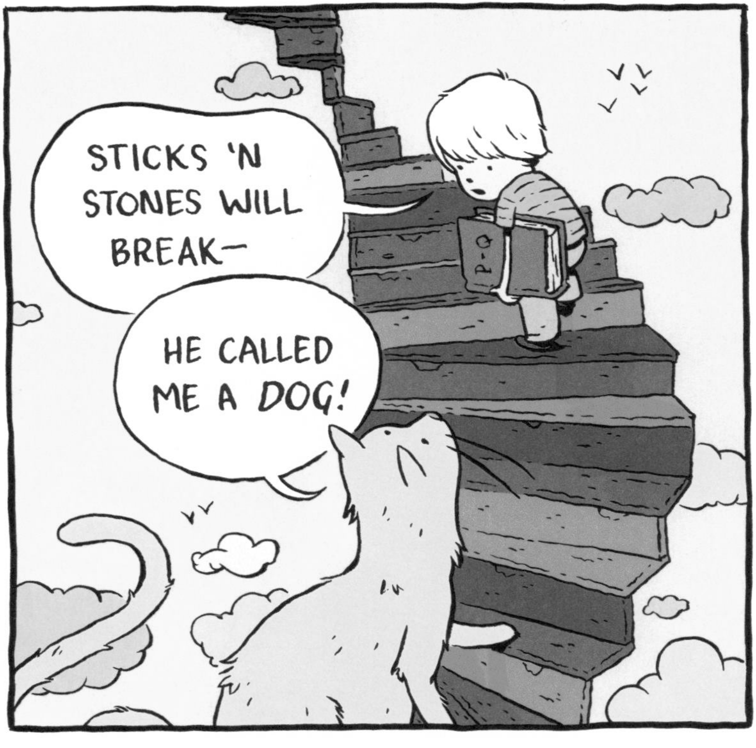
STICKS 'N STONES WILL BREAK—
HE CALLED ME A DOG!

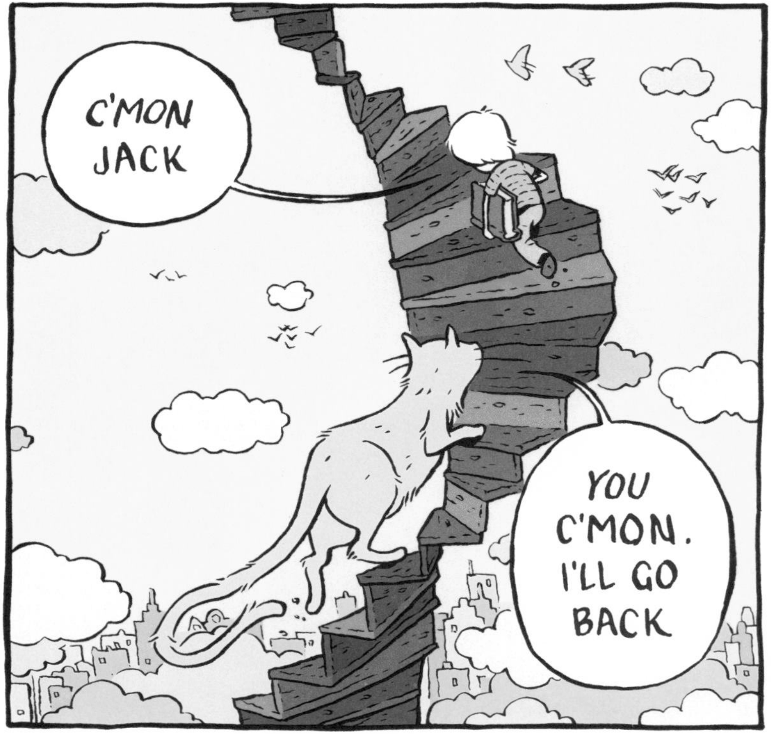
C'MON JACK
YOU C'MON. I'LL GO BACK

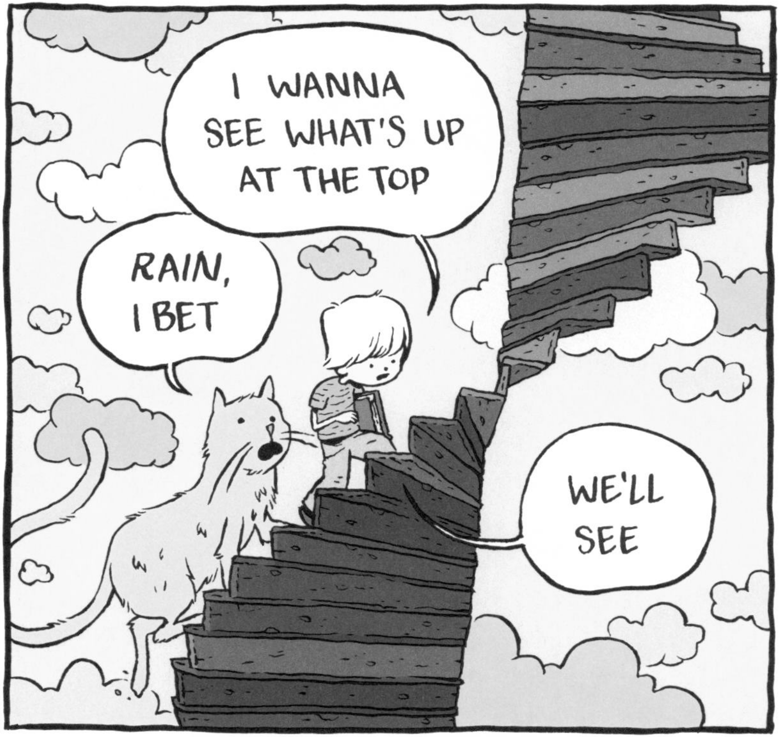
I WANNA SEE WHAT'S UP AT THE TOP
RAIN, I BET
WE'LL SEE

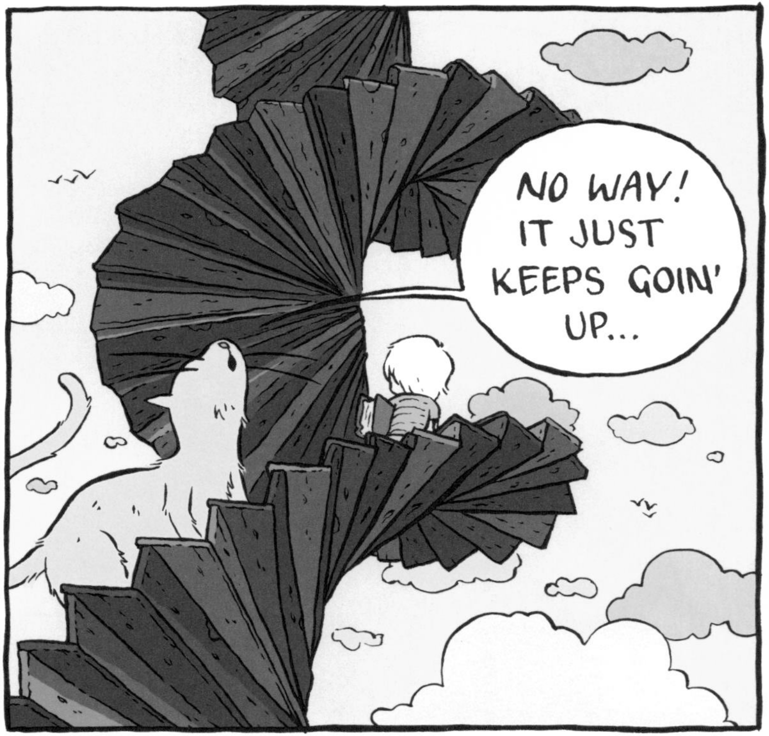
NO WAY! IT JUST KEEPS GOIN' UP...

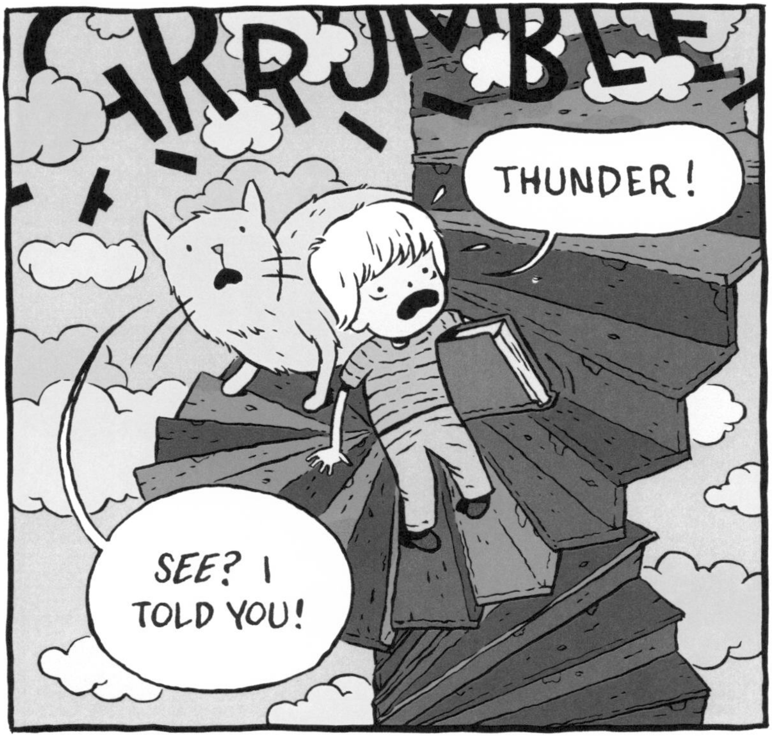
KRRUMBLE
THUNDER!
SEE? I TOLD YOU!

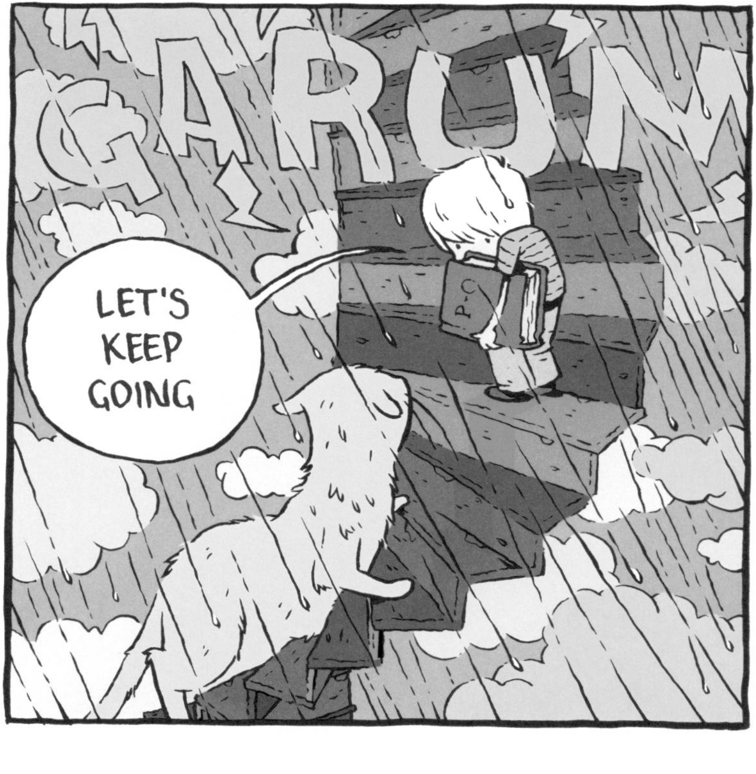

LET'S KEEP GOING

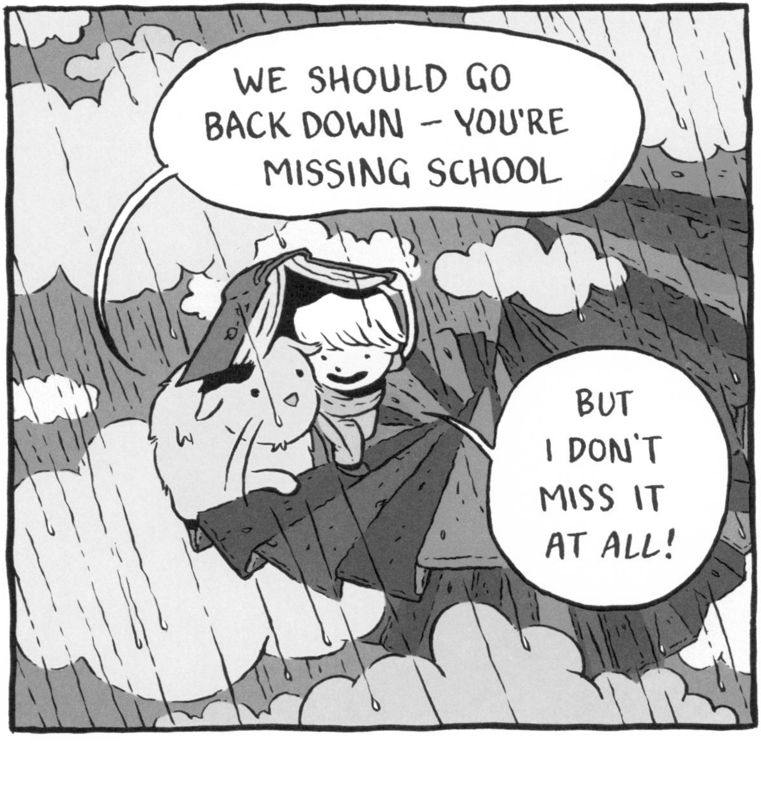
WE SHOULD GO BACK DOWN – YOU'RE MISSING SCHOOL
BUT I DON'T MISS IT AT ALL!

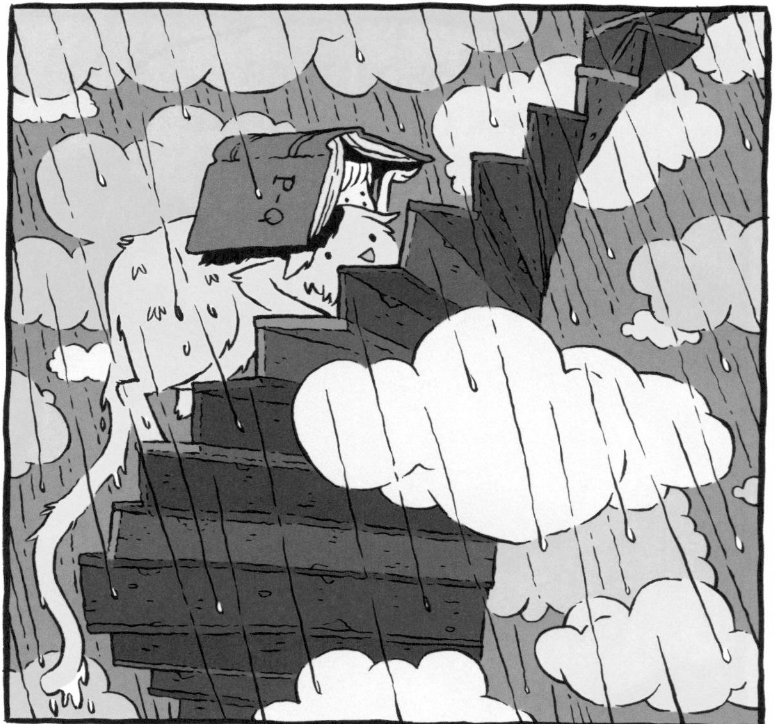
P-Q

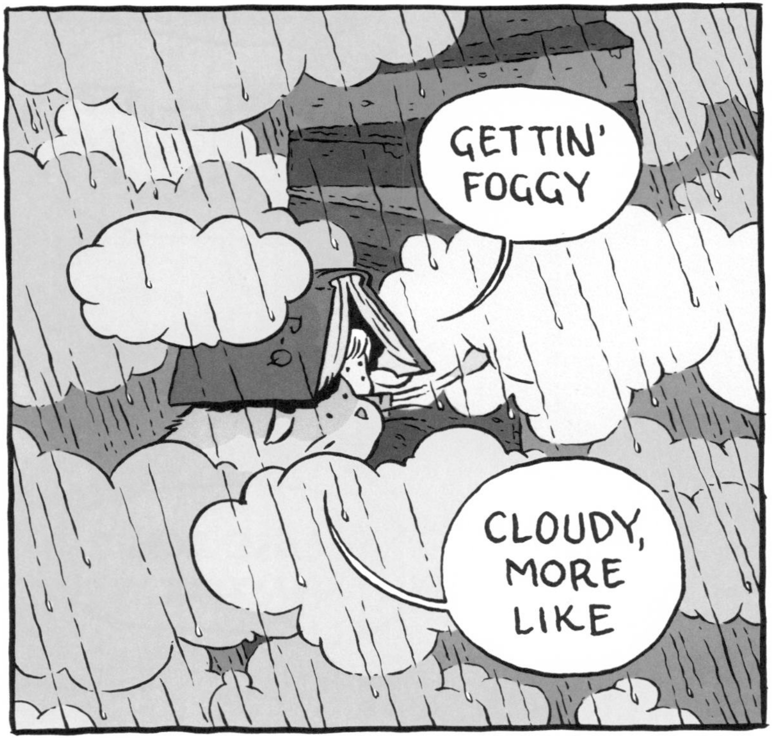
GETTIN' FOGGY
CLOUDY, MORE LIKE

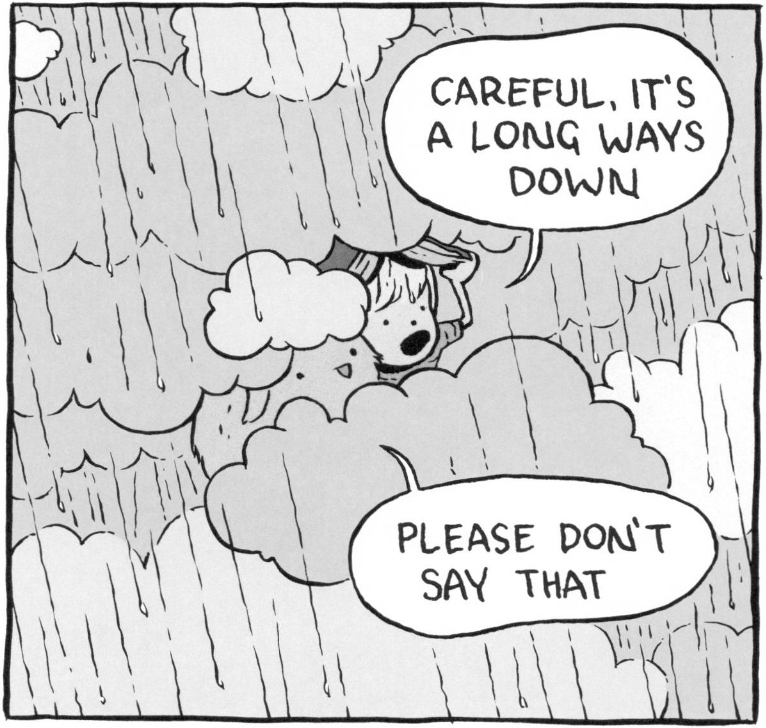
CAREFUL, IT'S A LONG WAYS DOWN
PLEASE DON'T SAY THAT

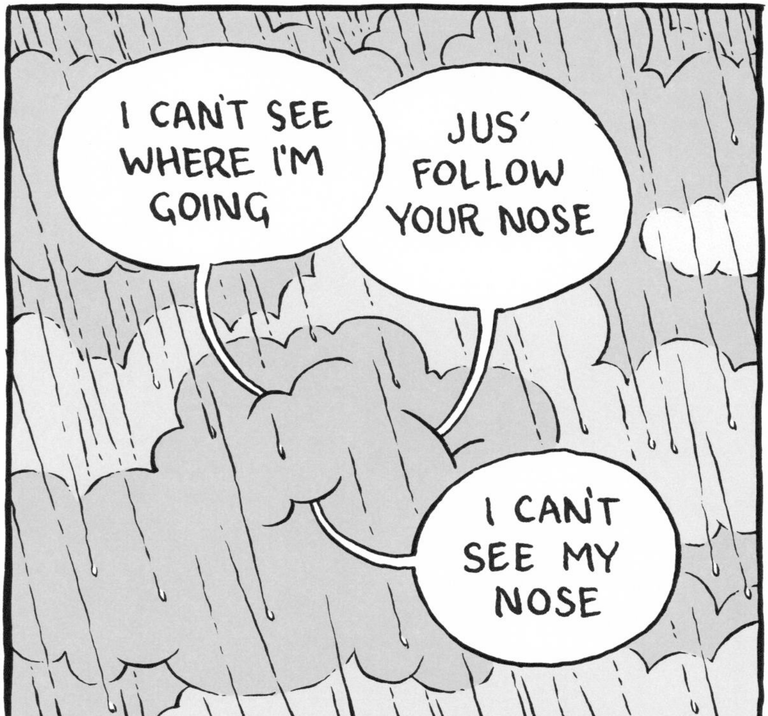
I CAN'T SEE WHERE I'M GOING
JUS' FOLLOW YOUR NOSE
I CAN'T SEE MY NOSE

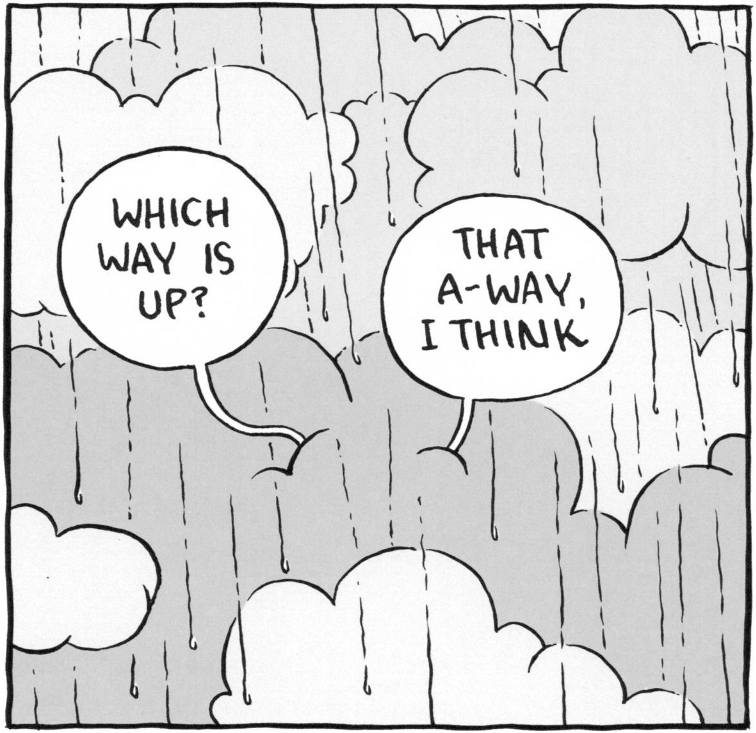
WHICH WAY IS UP?
THAT A-WAY, I THINK

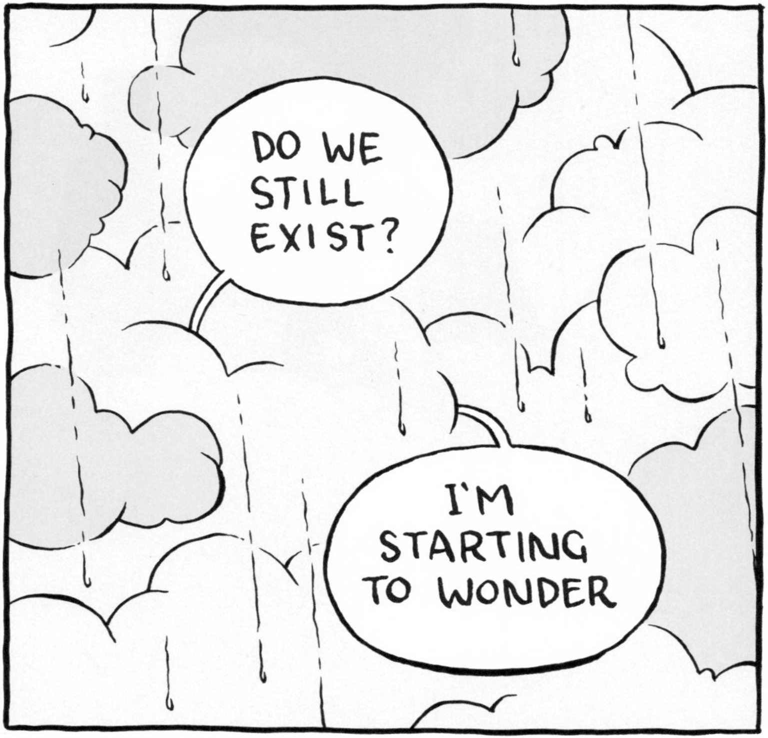
DO WE STILL EXIST?
I'M STARTING TO WONDER

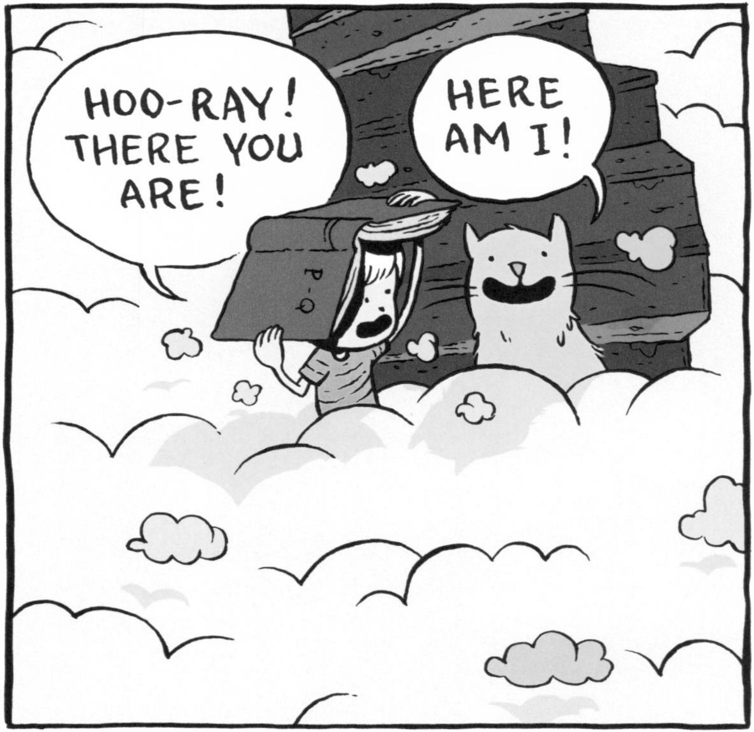
HOO-RAY! THERE YOU ARE!
P-Q
HERE AM I!

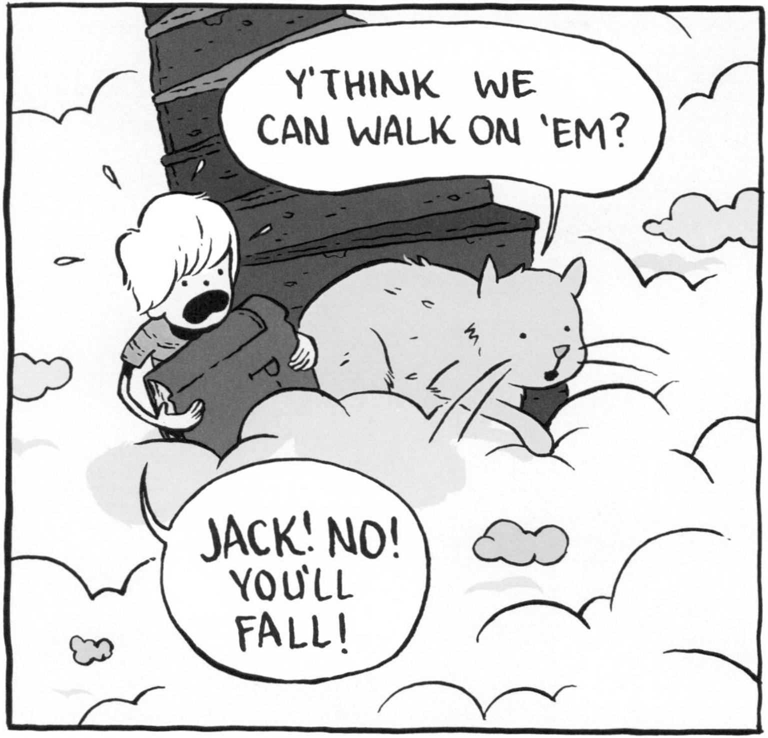
Y'THINK WE CAN WALK ON 'EM?
JACK! NO! YOU'LL FALL!

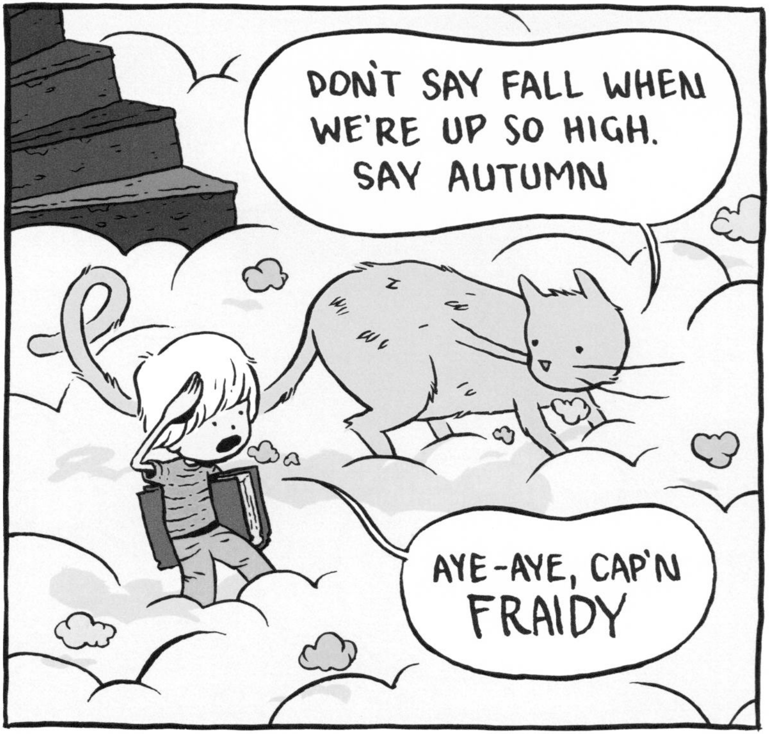
DON'T SAY FALL WHEN WE'RE UP SO HIGH. SAY AUTUMN
AYE-AYE, CAP'N FRAIDY

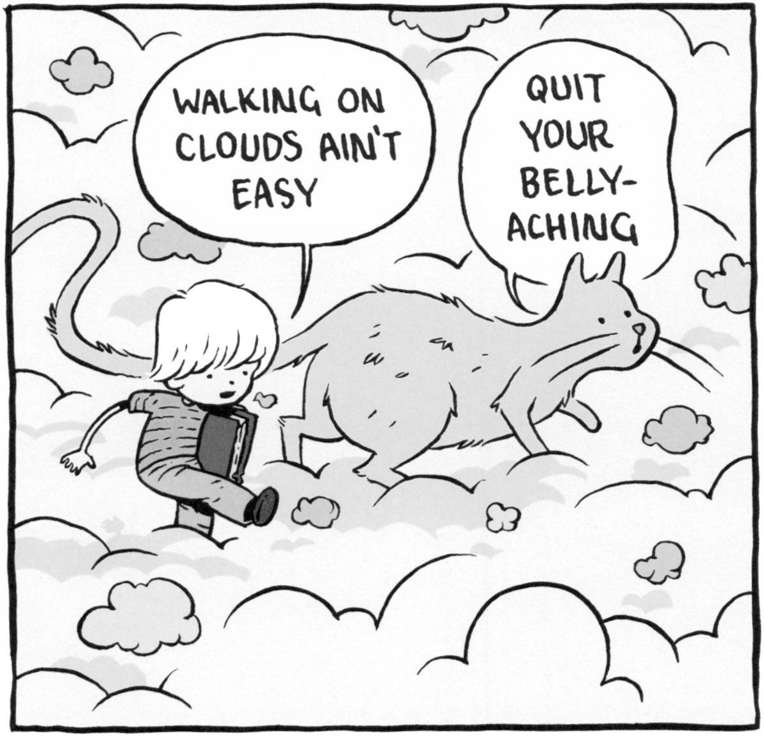
WALKING ON CLOUDS AIN'T EASY
QUIT YOUR BELLY-ACHING

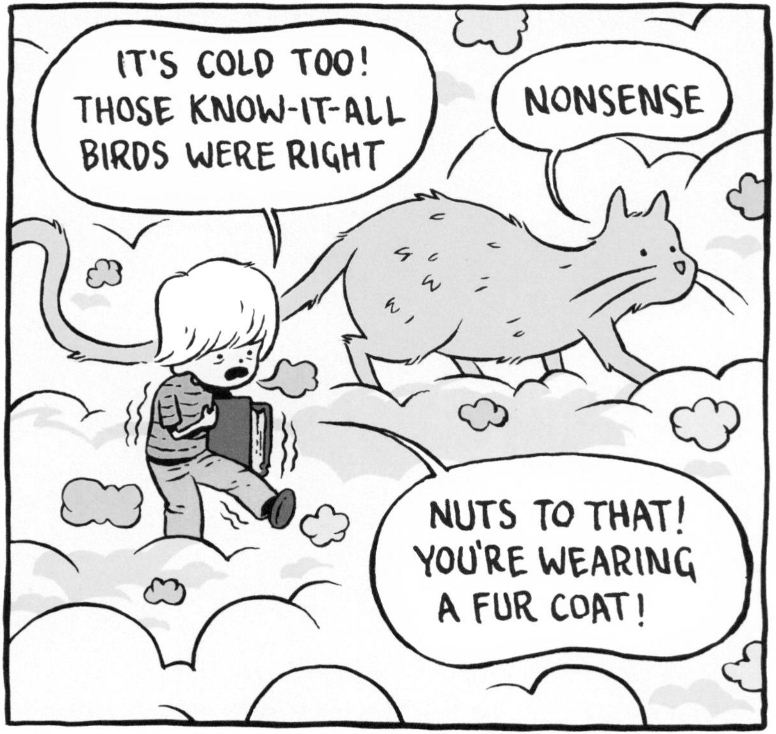
IT'S COLD TOO! THOSE KNOW-IT-ALL BIRDS WERE RIGHT
NONSENSE
NUTS TO THAT! YOU'RE WEARING A FUR COAT!

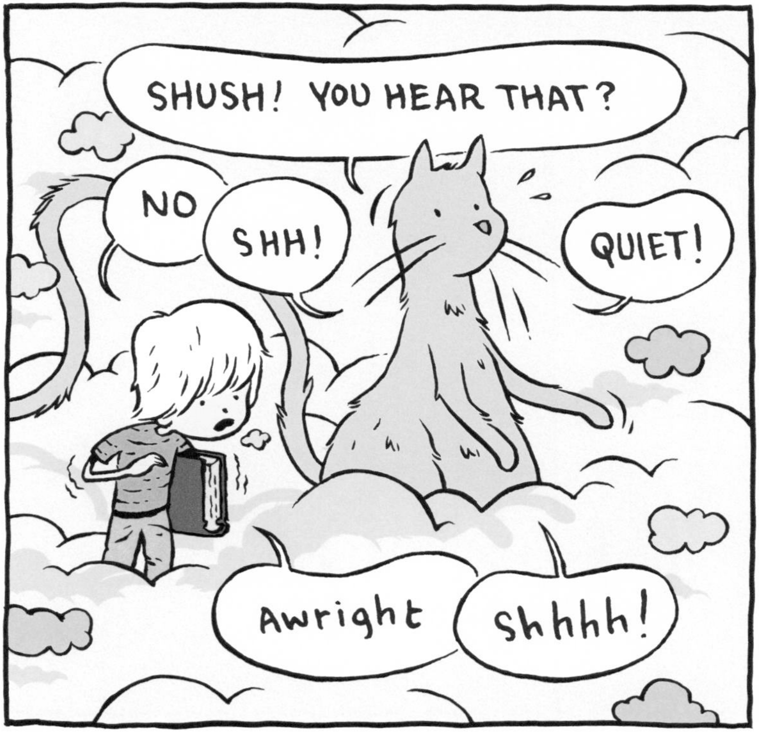
SHUSH! YOU HEAR THAT?
NO
SHH!
QUIET!
Awright
Shhhh!

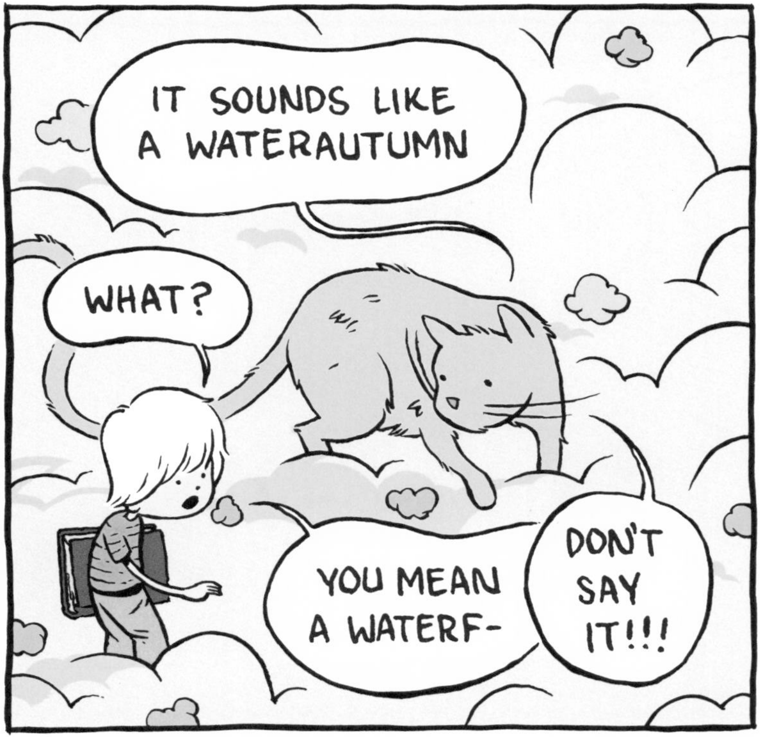
IT SOUNDS LIKE A WATERAUTUMN
WHAT?
YOU MEAN A WATERF-
DON'T SAY IT!!!

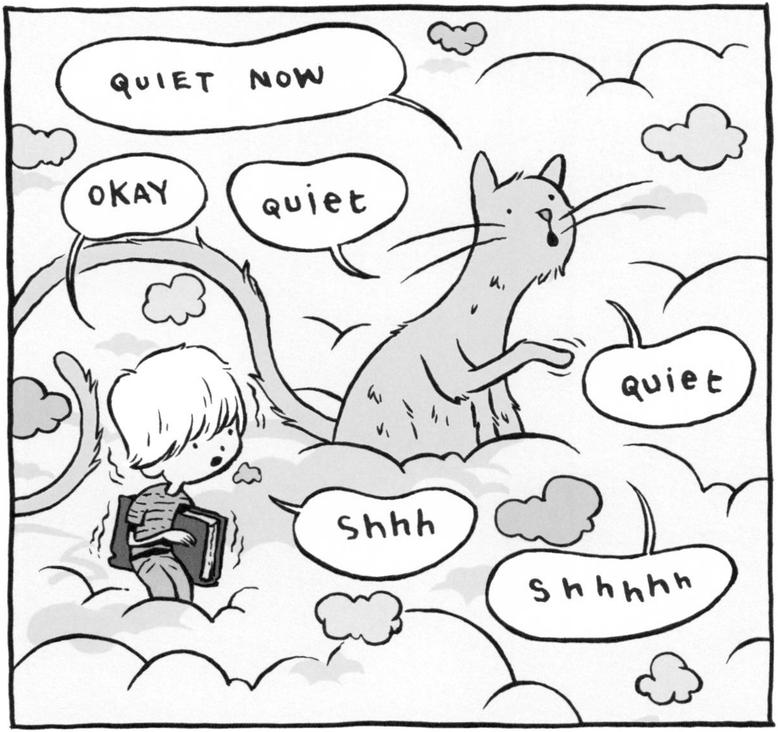
QUIET NOW
OKAY
quiet
quiet
Shhh
Shhhhh

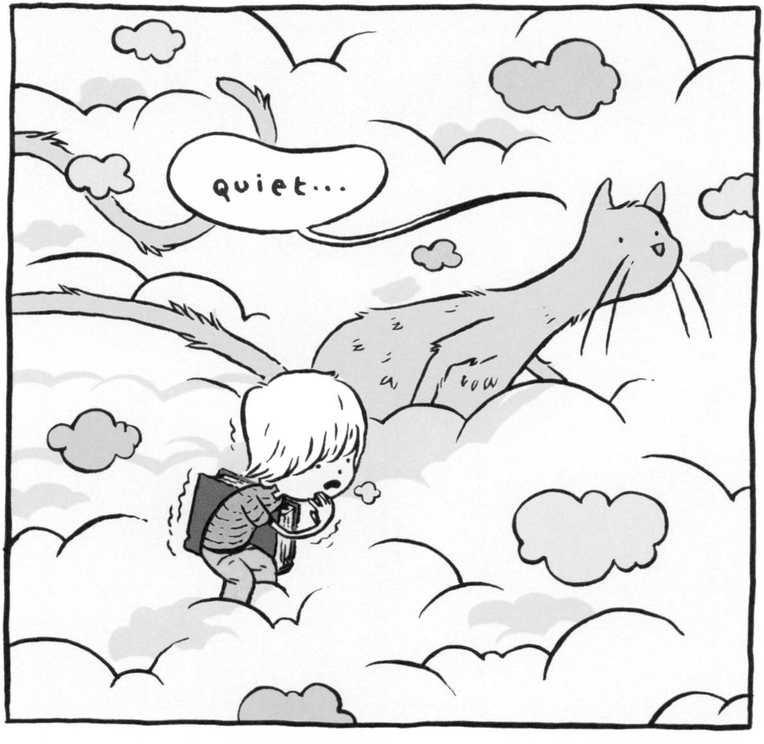
quiet...

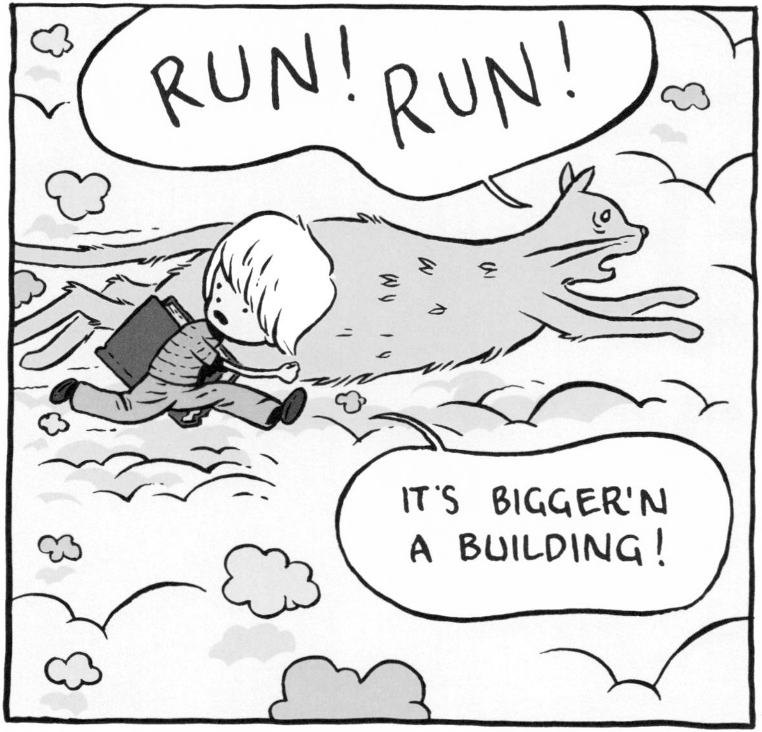
RUN! RUN!
IT'S BIGGER'N A BUILDING!

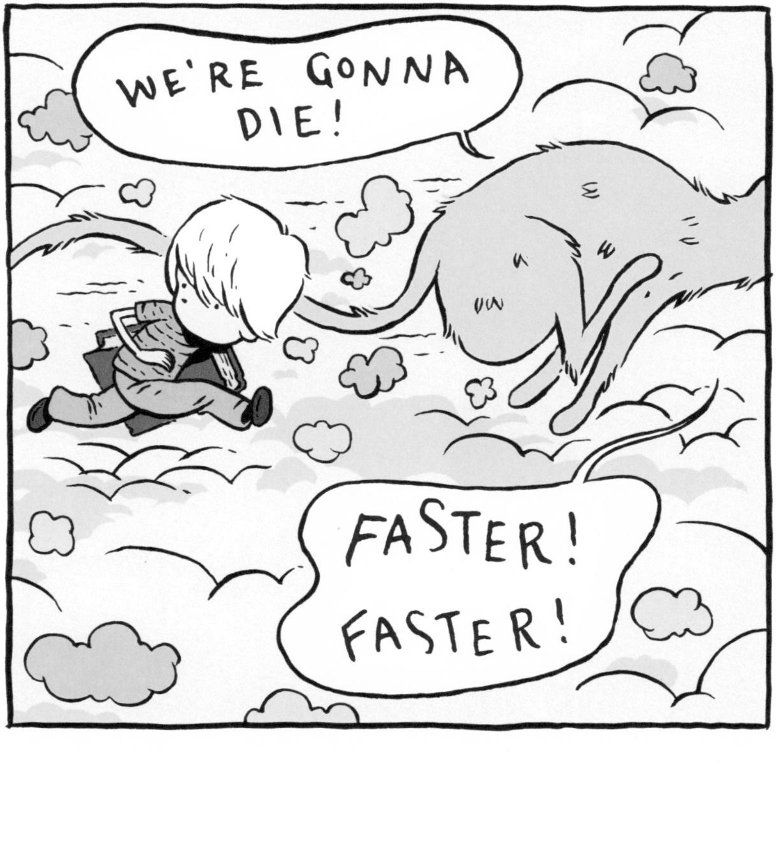
WE'RE GONNA DIE!
FASTER! FASTER!

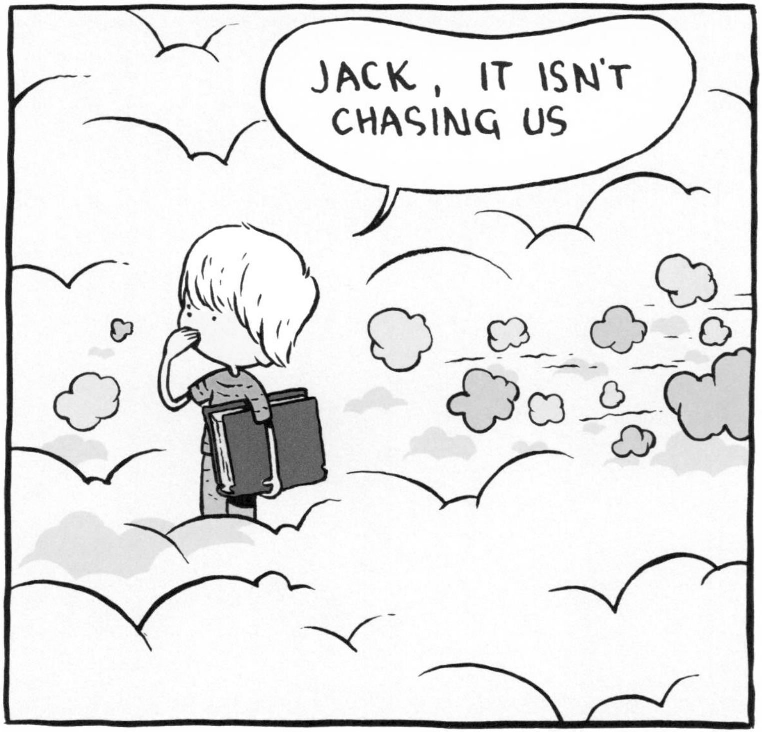
JACK, IT ISN'T CHASING US

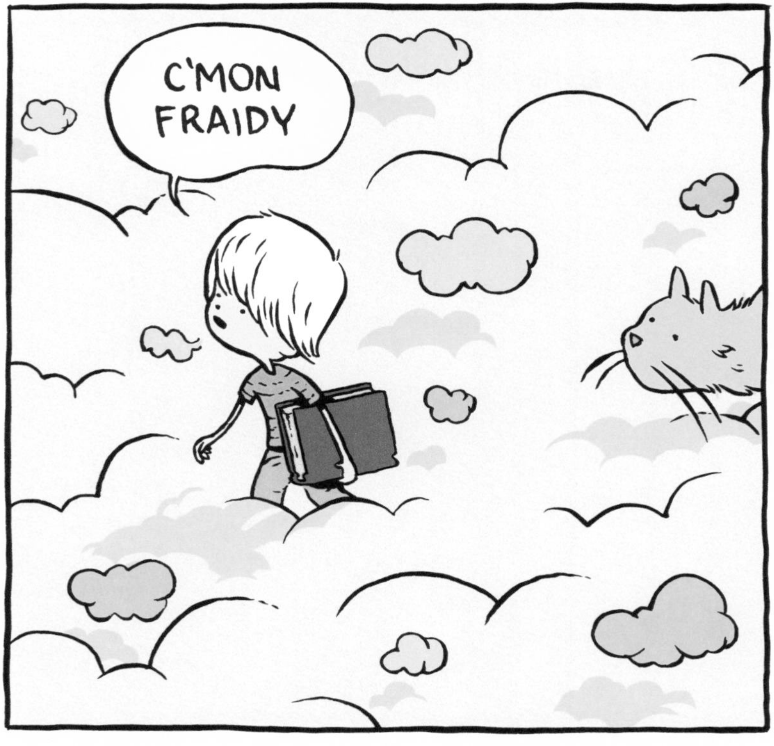
C'MON FRAIDY

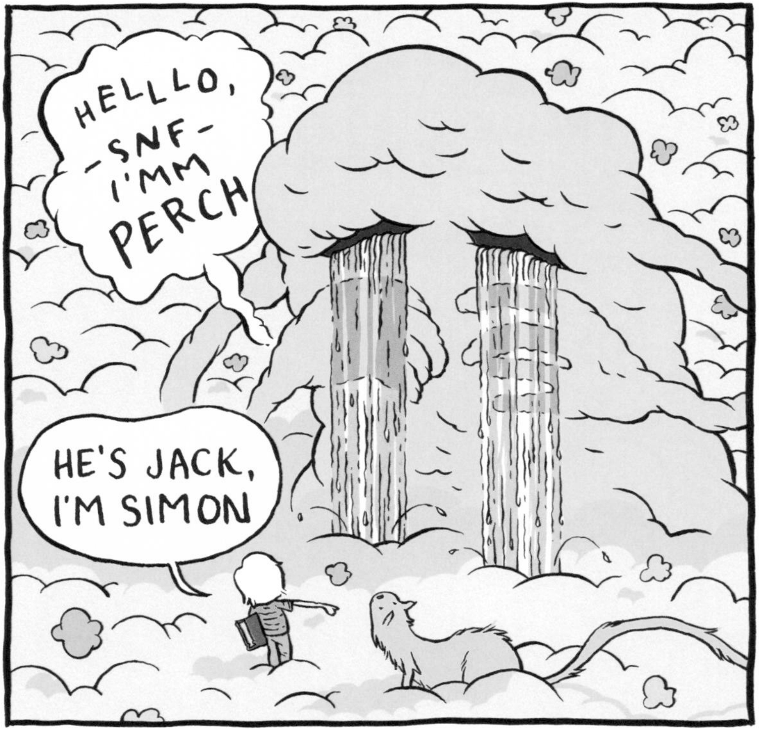
HELLLO, -SNF- I'MM PERCH
HE'S JACK, I'M SIMON

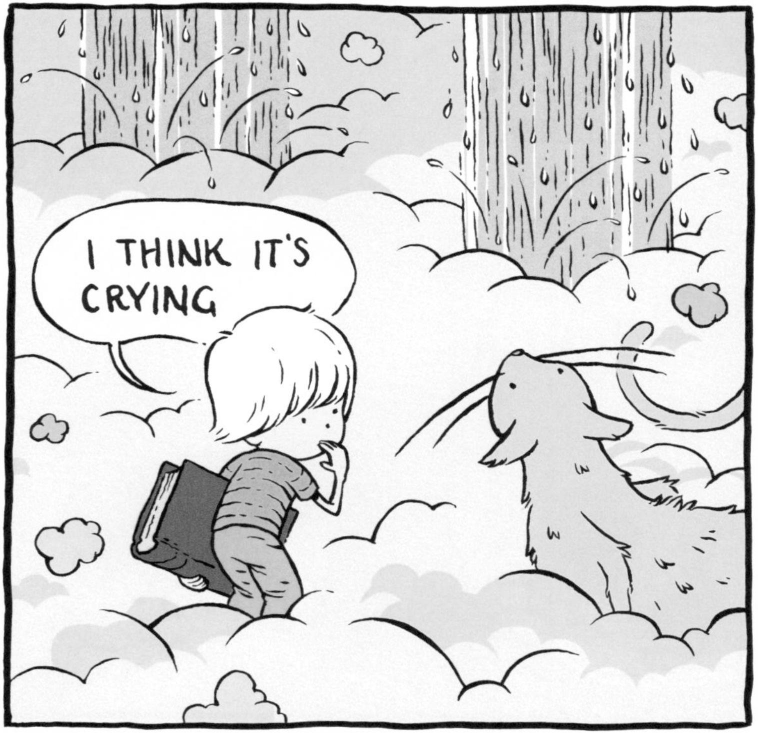
I THINK IT'S CRYING

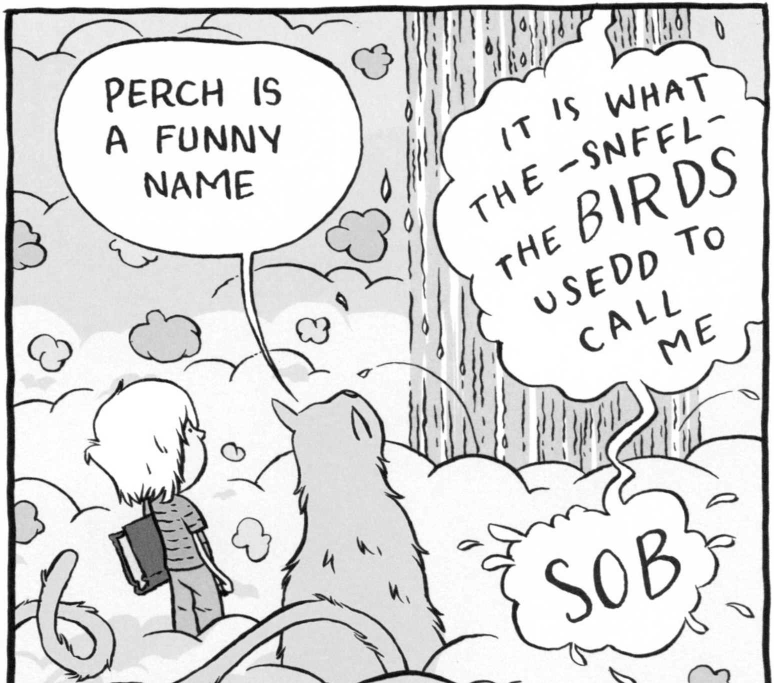
PERCH IS A FUNNY NAME
IT IS WHAT THE -SNFFL- THE BIRDS USEDD TO CALL ME
SOB

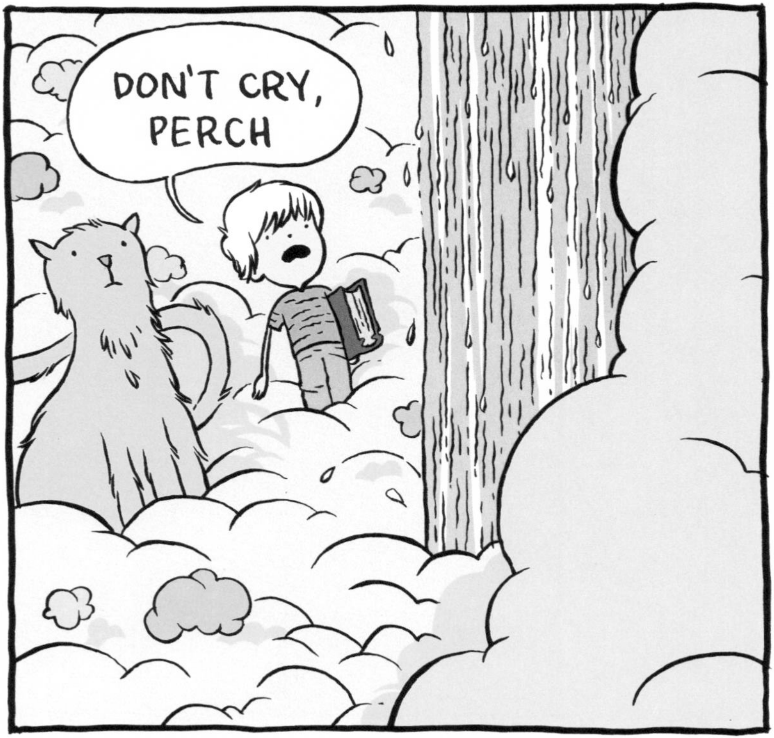
DON'T CRY, PERCH

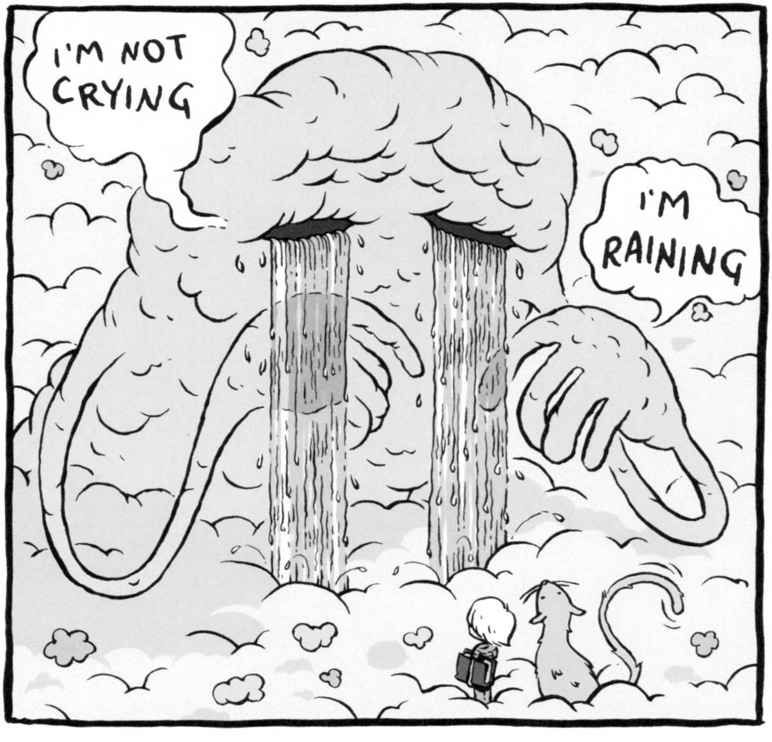
I'M NOT CRYING
I'M RAINING

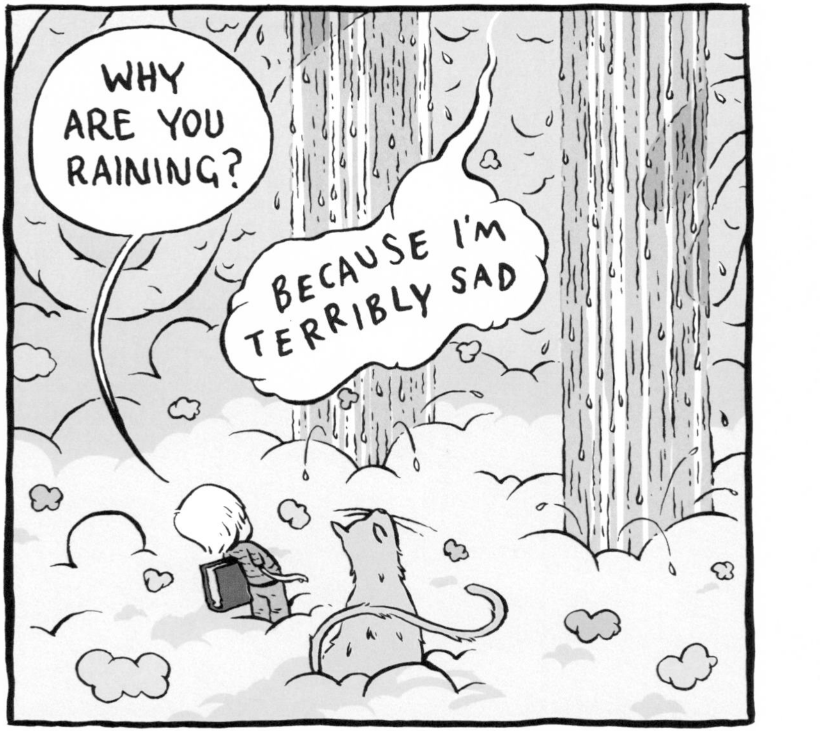
WHY ARE YOU RAINING?
BECAUSE I'M TERRIBLY SAD

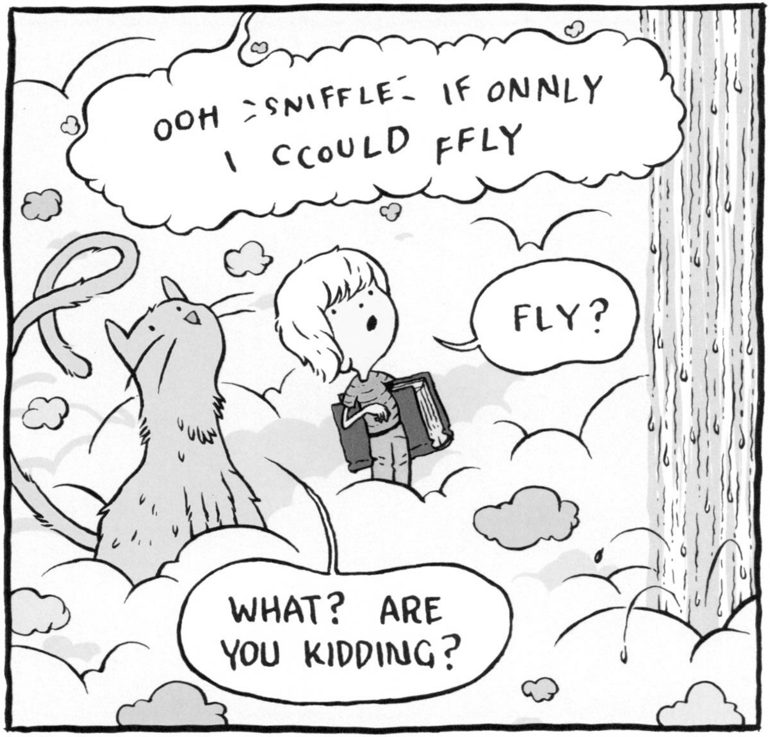
OOH ~SNIFFLE~ IF ONNLY I CCOULD FFLY
FLY?
WHAT? ARE YOU KIDDING?

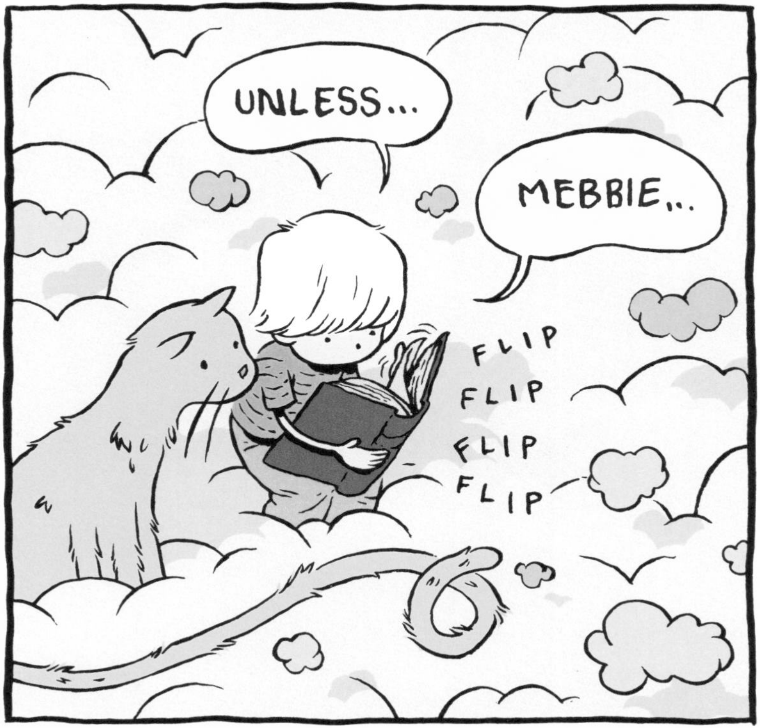
UNLESS...
MEBBIE...
FLIP
FLIP
FLIP
FLIP

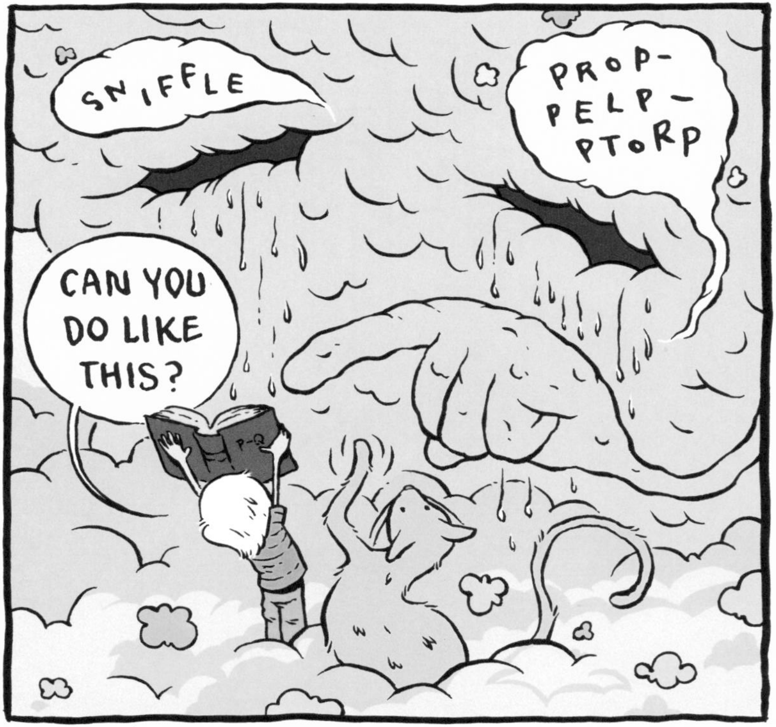
SNIFFLE
PROP-PELP-PTORP
CAN YOU DO LIKE THIS?
P-Q

PROPPO
PROP-
LOPPA-
DORO
YES! A
PROPELLER!
SPIN!
SPIN!

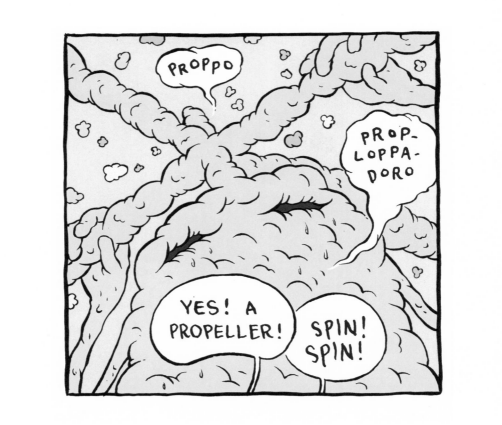

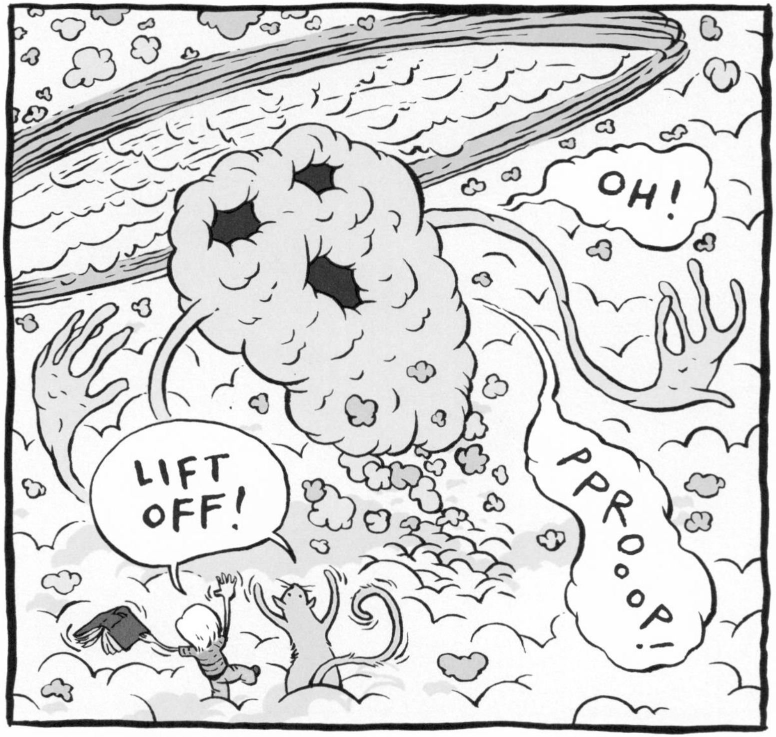
OH!
PPROOOP!!
LIFT OFF!

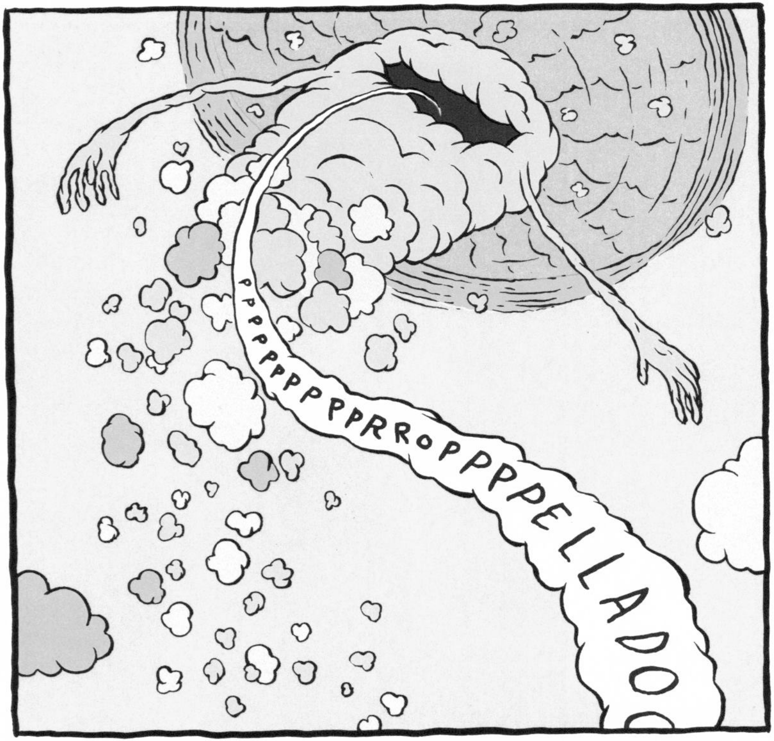
PPPPPPPPPPRRRoPPPPELLADO

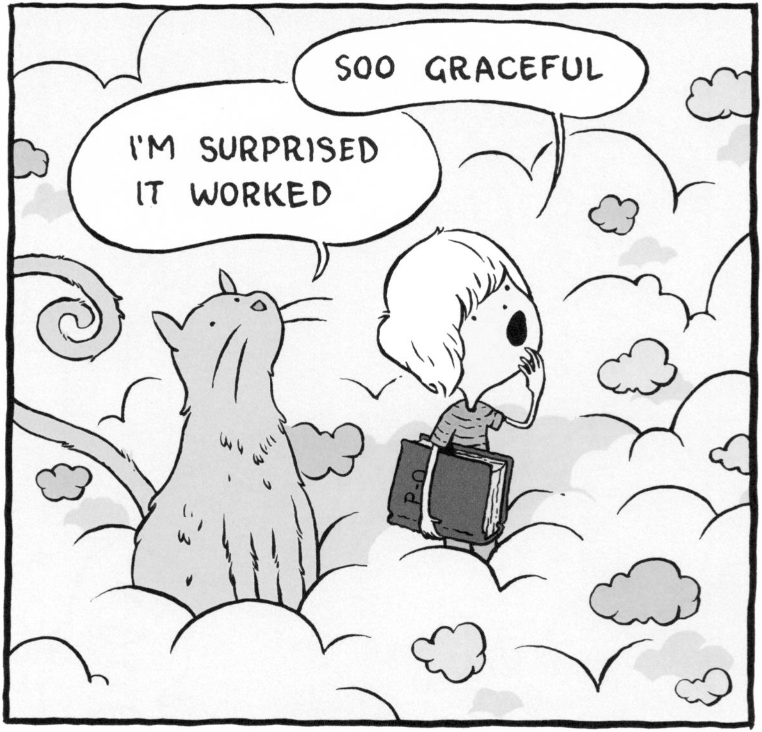
I'M SURPRISED IT WORKED
SOO GRACEFUL
P-O

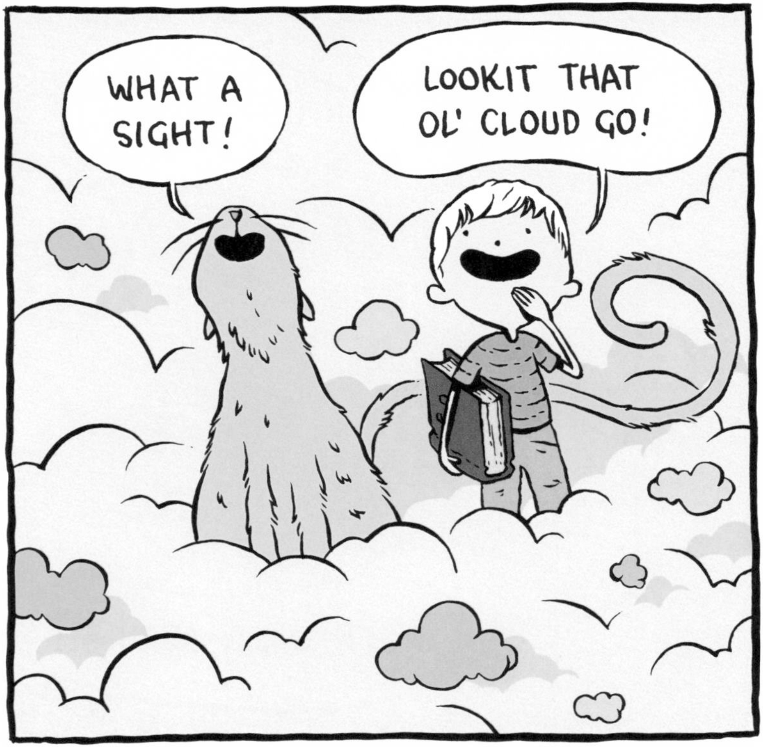
WHAT A SIGHT!
LOOKIT THAT OL' CLOUD GO!

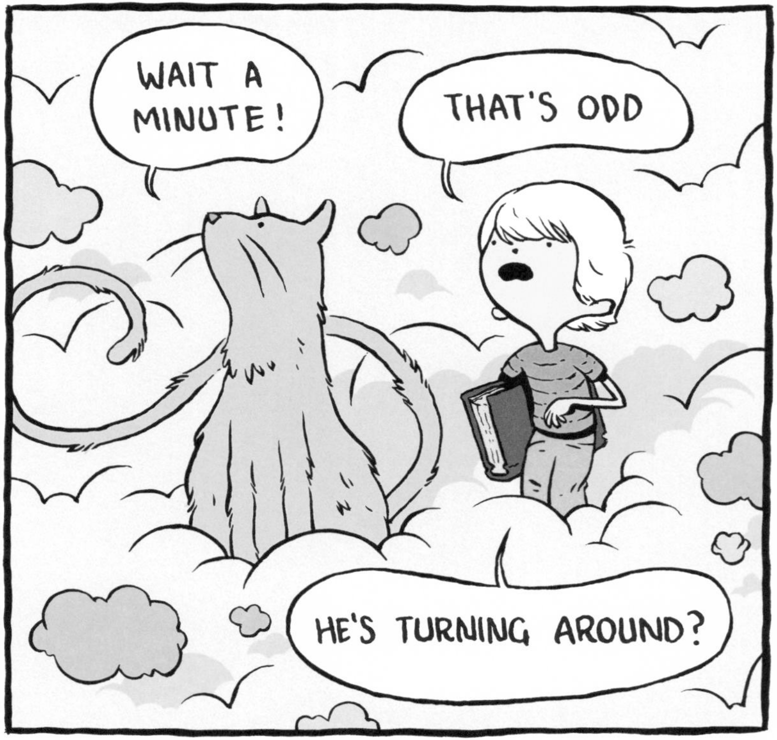
WAIT A MINUTE!
THAT'S ODD
HE'S TURNING AROUND?

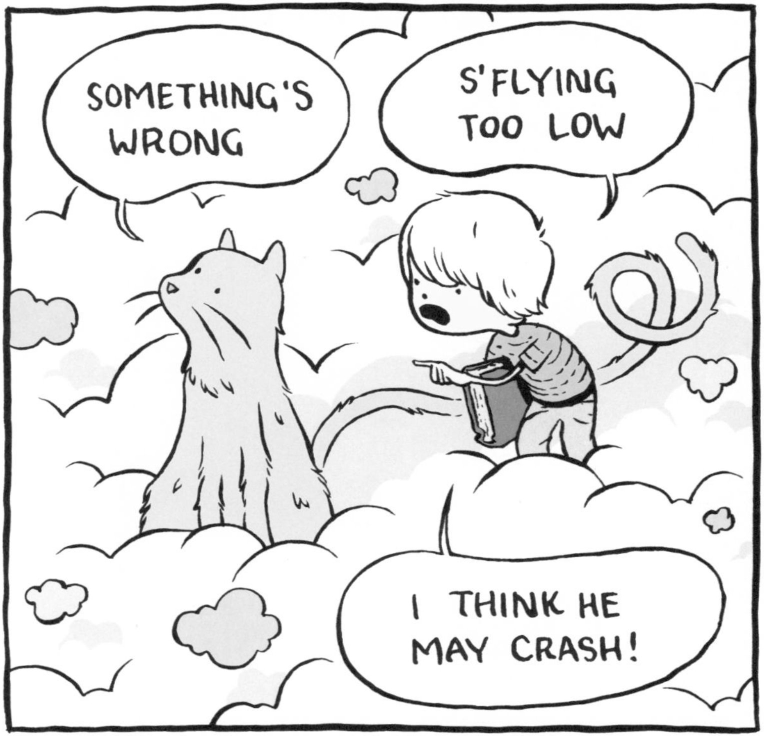
SOMETHING'S WRONG
S'FLYING TOO LOW
I THINK HE MAY CRASH!

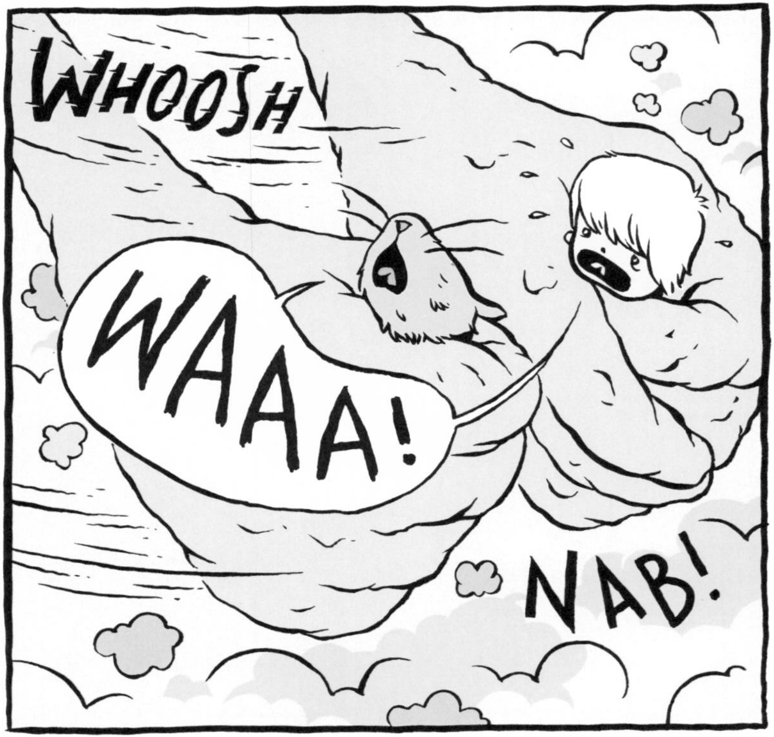
WHOOSH
WAAAA!
NAB!

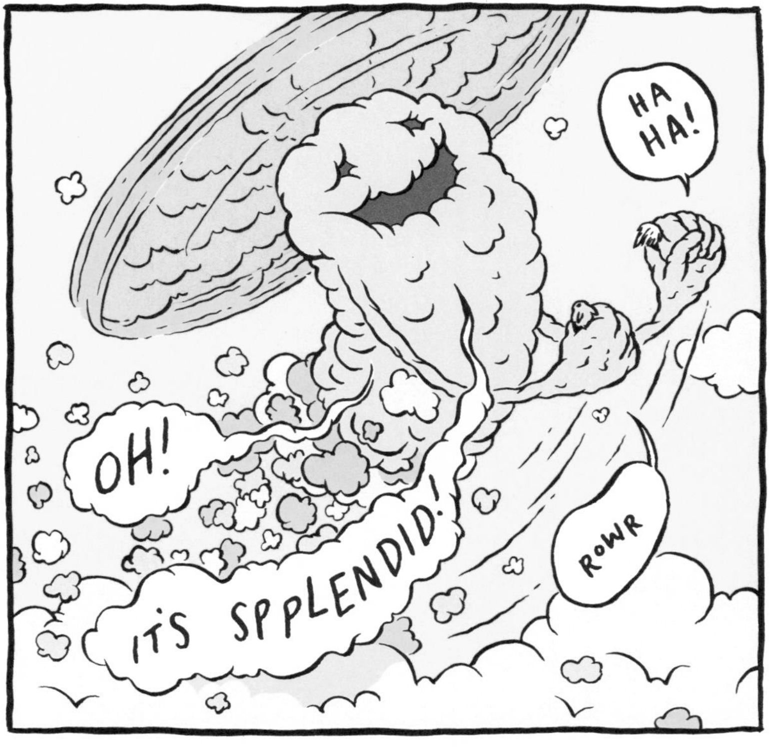
HA HA!
OH!
IT'S SPPLENDID!
ROWR

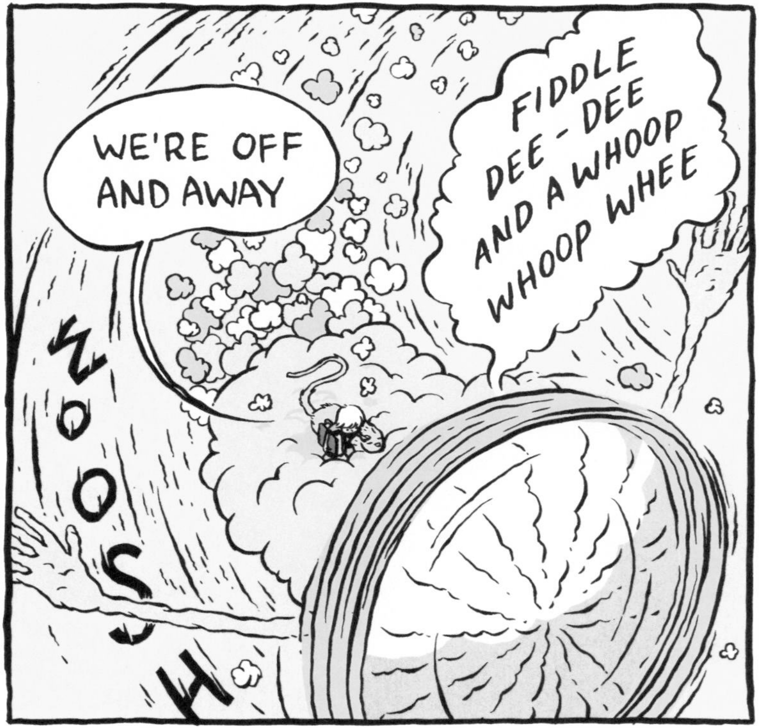
WE'RE OFF AND AWAY
FIDDLE DEE-DEE AND A WHOOP WHOOP WHEE
WOOSH

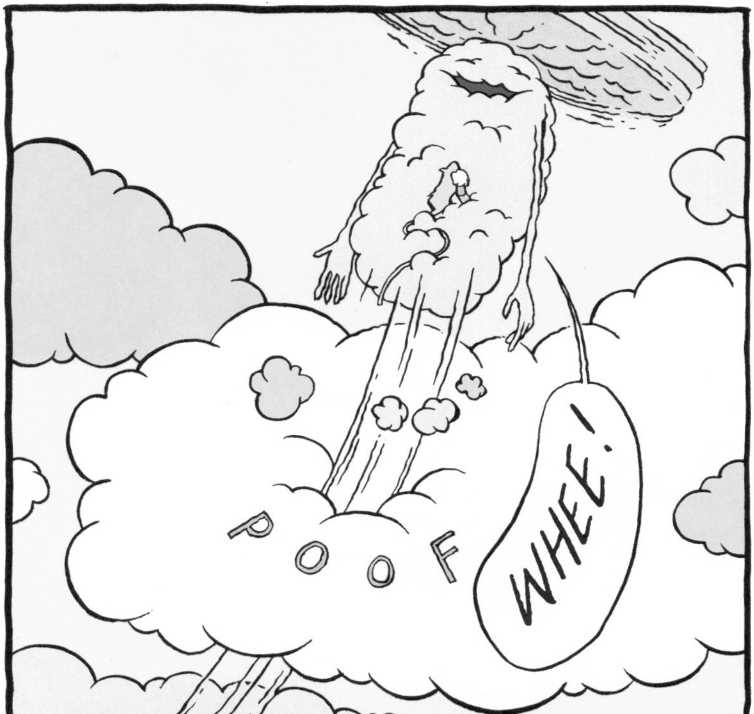
POOF
WHEE!

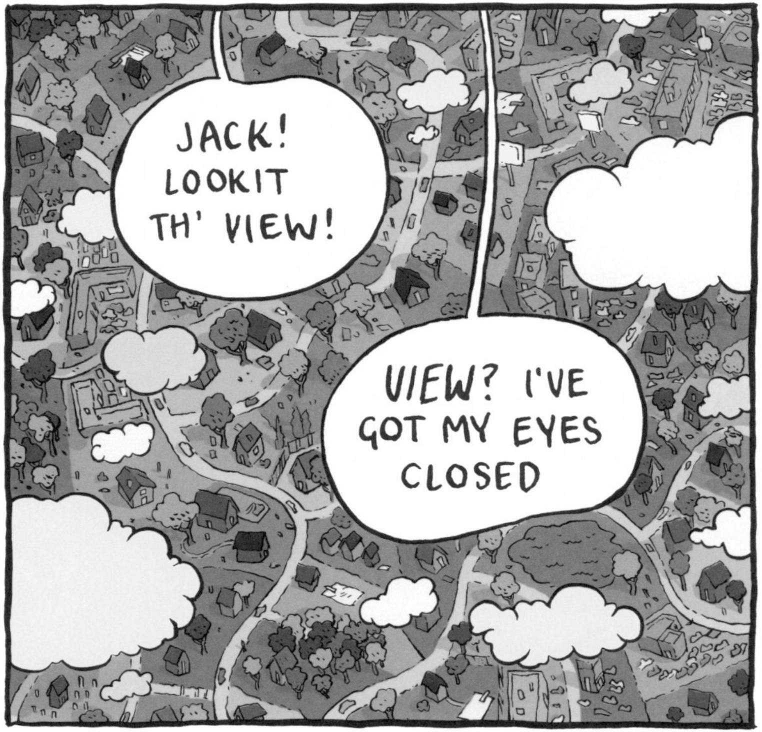
JACK! LOOKIT TH' VIEW!
VIEW? I'VE GOT MY EYES CLOSED

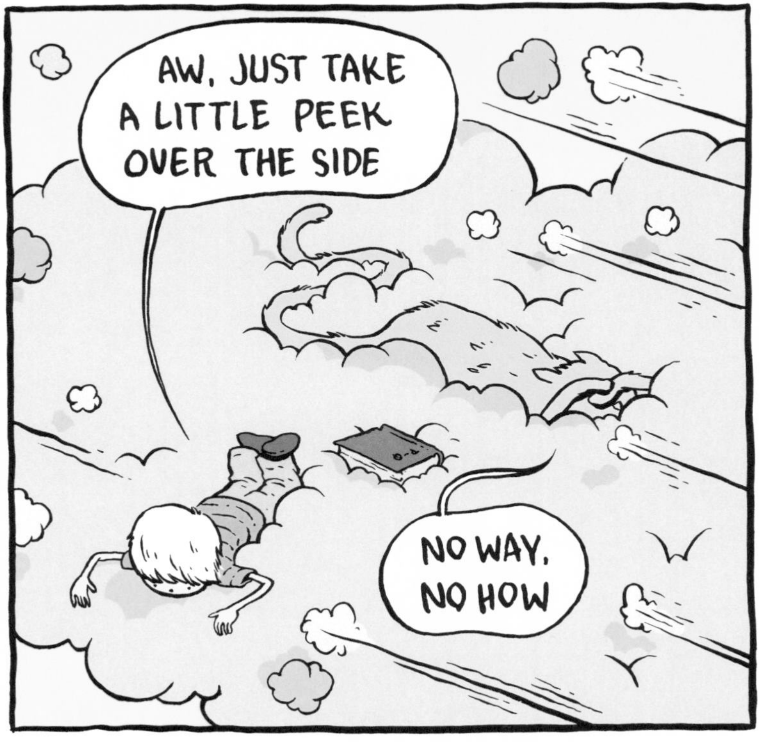
AW, JUST TAKE A LITTLE PEEK OVER THE SIDE
NO WAY, NO HOW

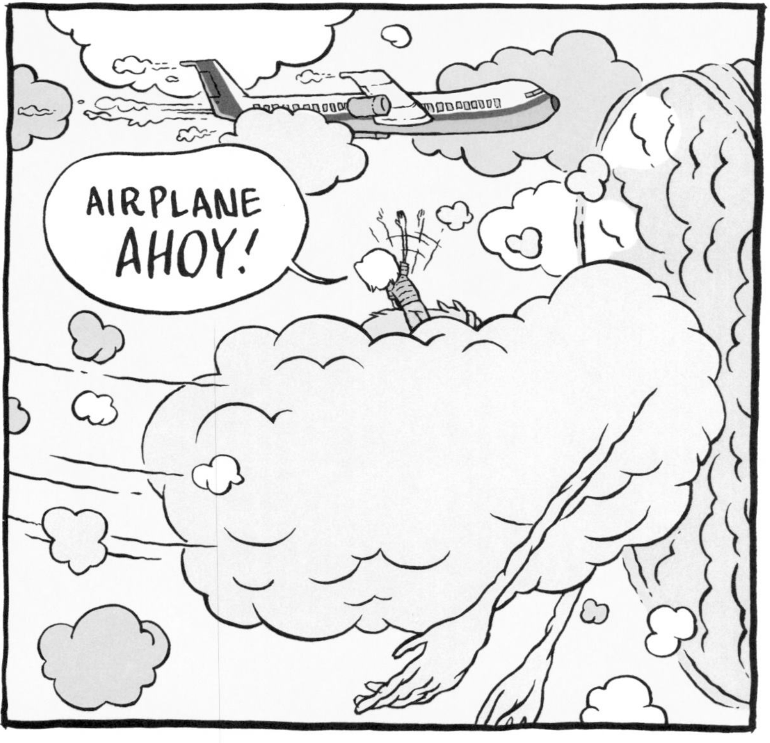
AIRPLANE AHOY!

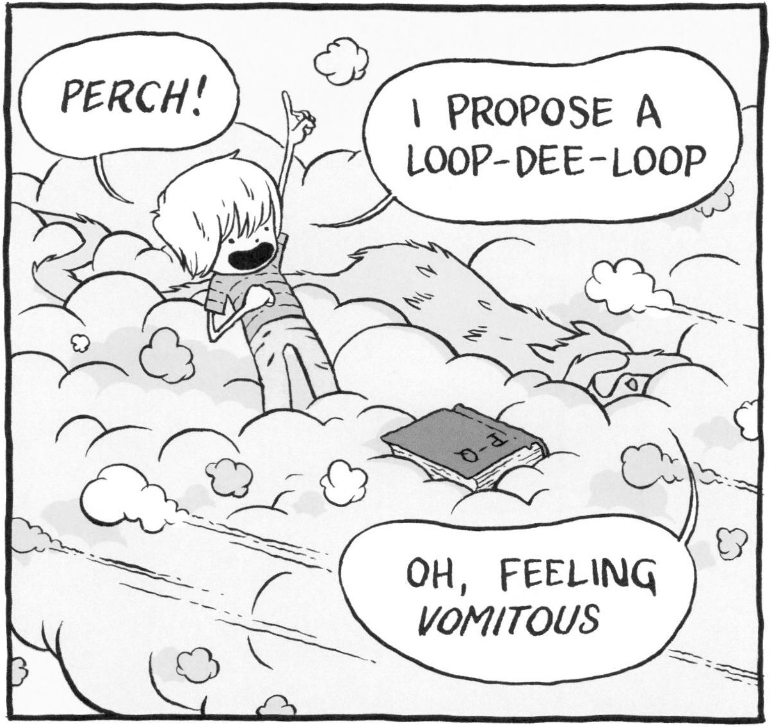
PERCH!
I PROPOSE A LOOP-DEE-LOOP
OH, FEELING *VOMITOUS*

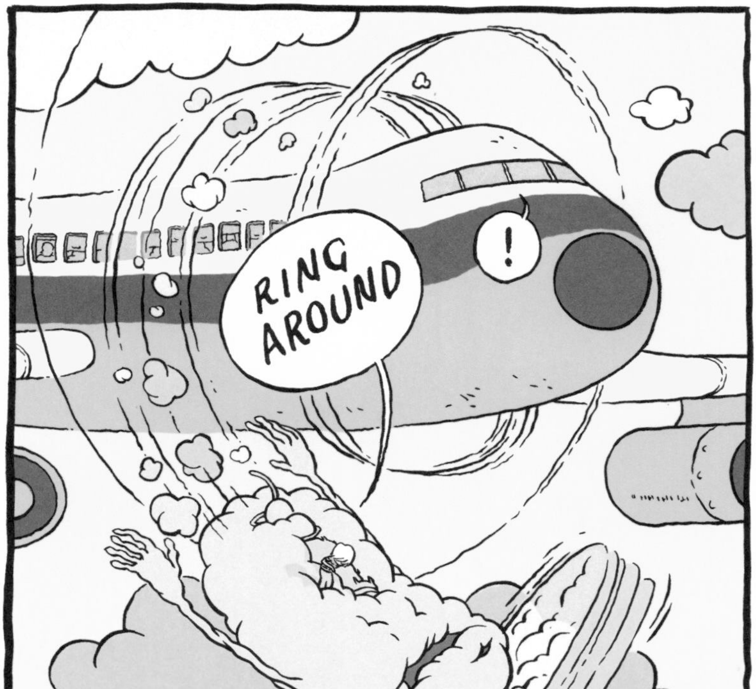
RING AROUND
!

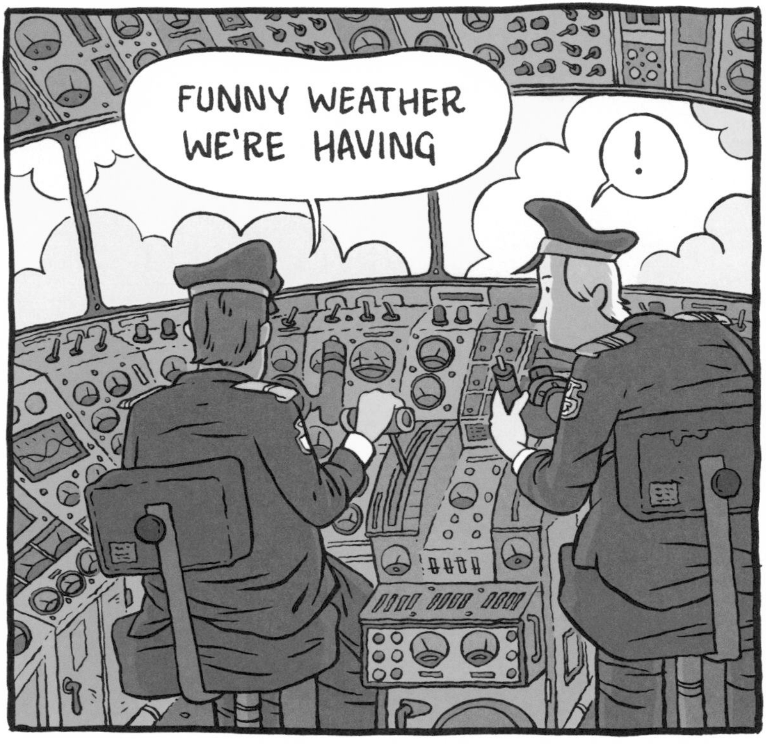
FUNNY WEATHER WE'RE HAVING
!

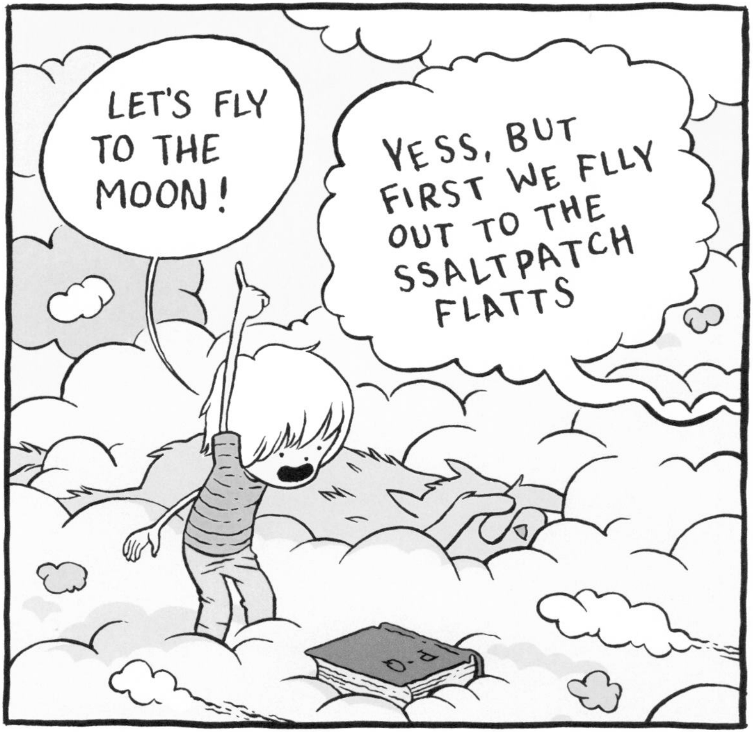
LET'S FLY TO THE MOON!
YESS, BUT FIRST WE FLLY OUT TO THE SSALTPATCH FLATTS
R.O

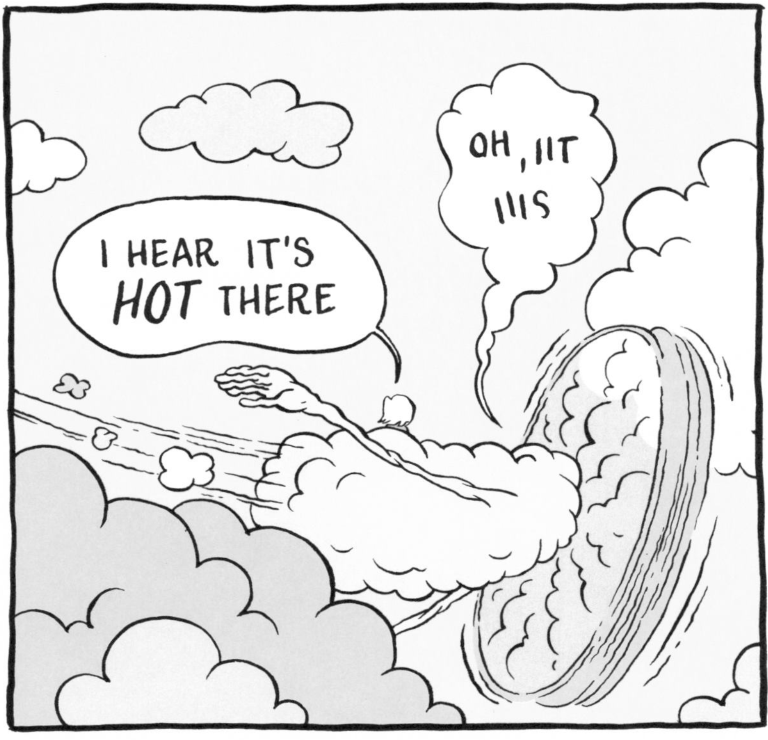
I HEAR IT'S *HOT* THERE
OH, IIT IIIS

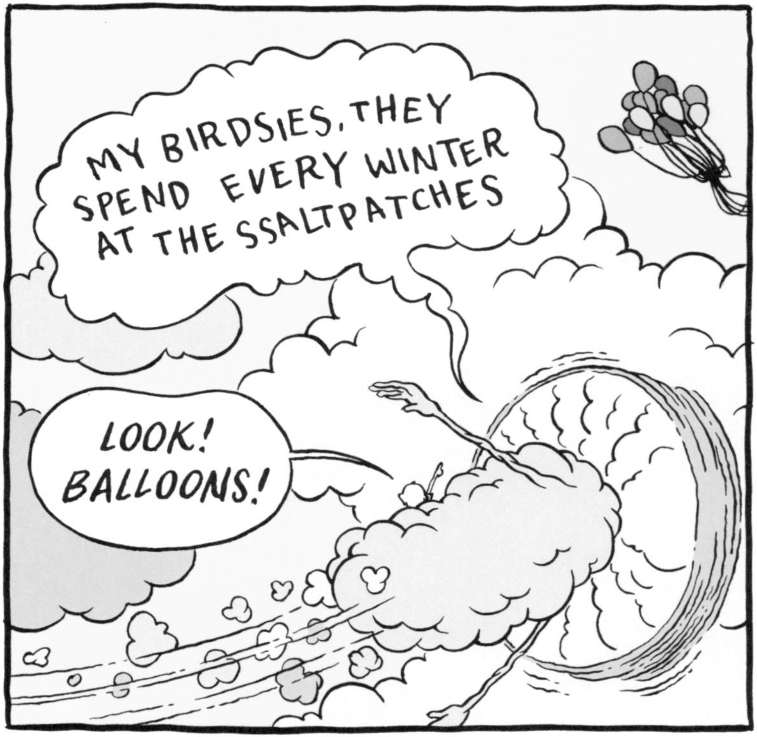
MY BIRDSIES, THEY SPEND EVERY WINTER AT THE SSALTPATCHES
LOOK! BALLOONS!

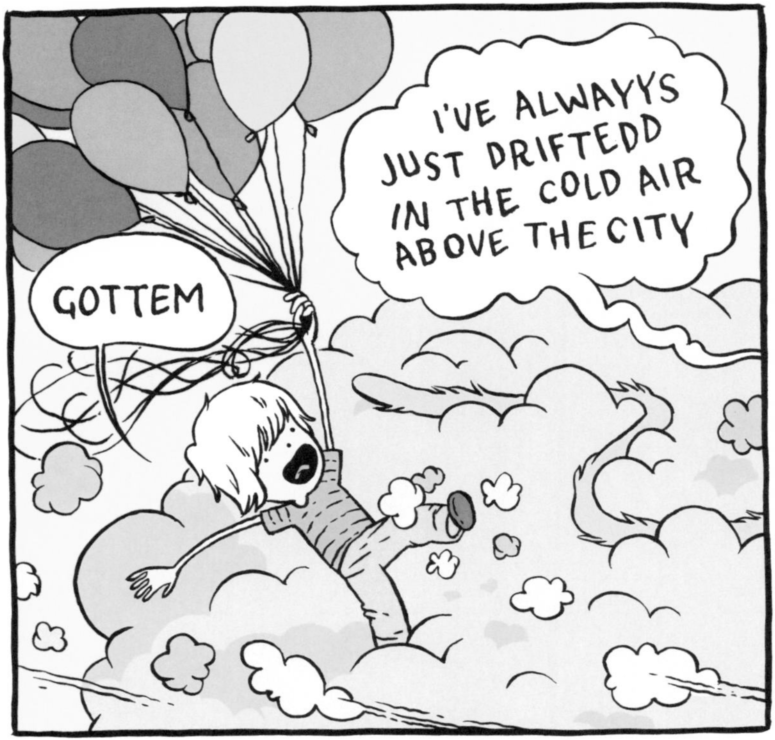
GOTTEM
I'VE ALWAYYS JUST DRIFTEDD IN THE COLD AIR ABOVE THE CITY

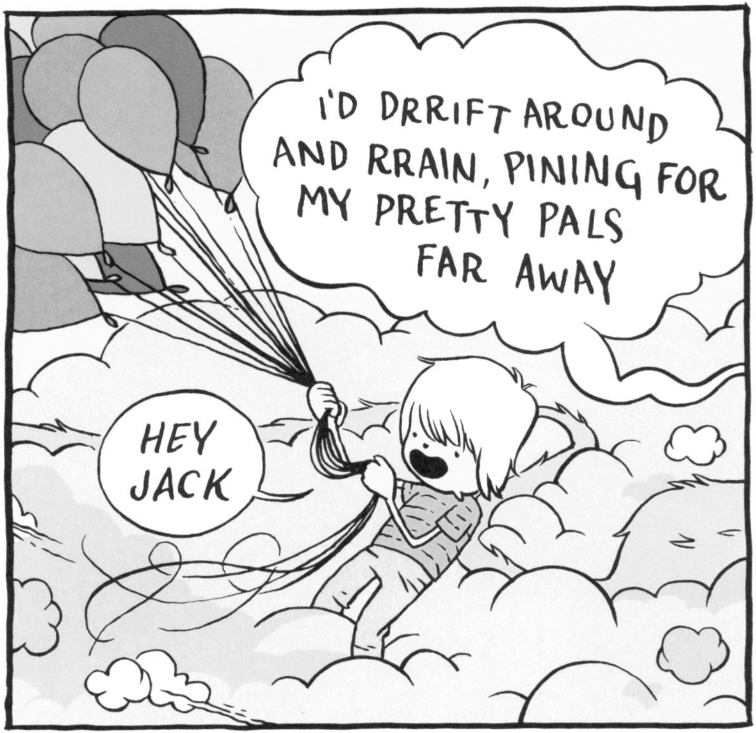
I'D DRRIFT AROUND AND RRAIN, PINING FOR MY PRETTY PALS FAR AWAY
HEY JACK

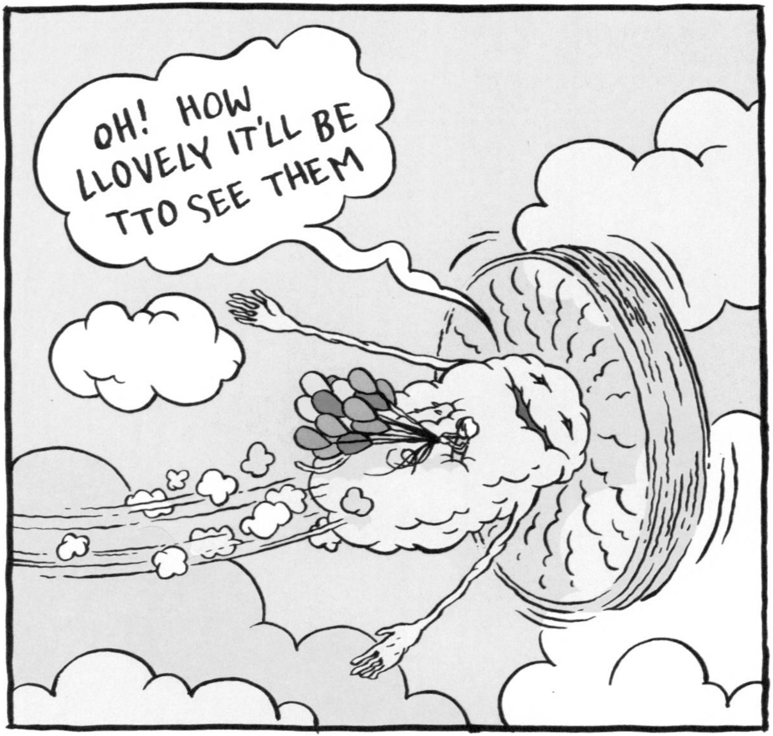
OH! HOW LLOVELY IT'LL BE TTO SEE THEM

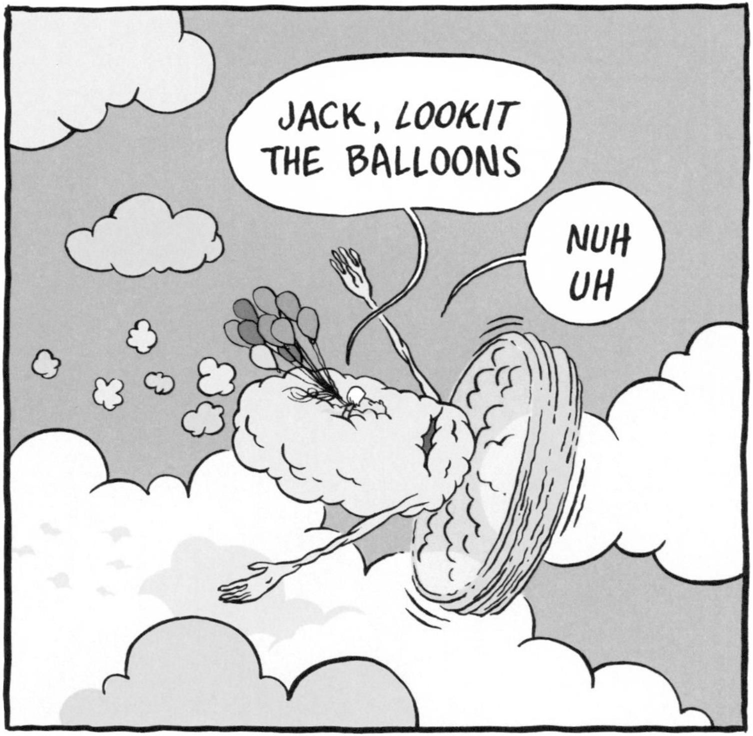
JACK, LOOKIT THE BALLOONS
NUH UH

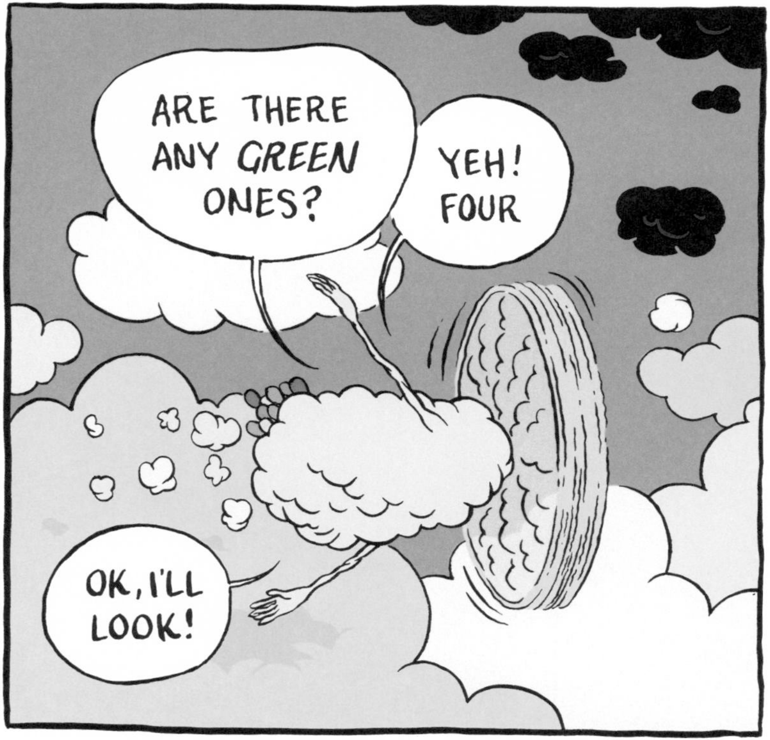
ARE THERE ANY GREEN ONES?
YEH! FOUR
OK, I'LL LOOK!

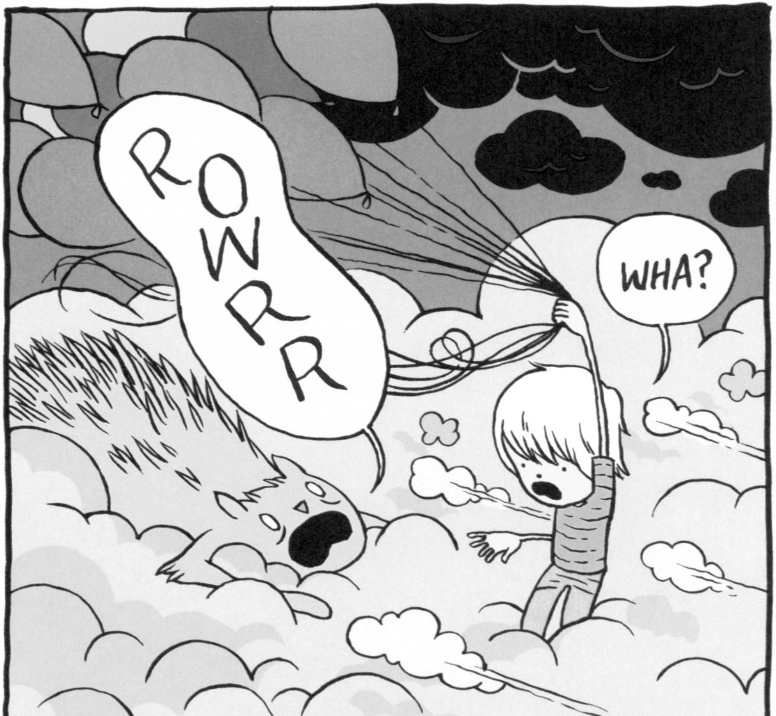
ROWRR
WHA?

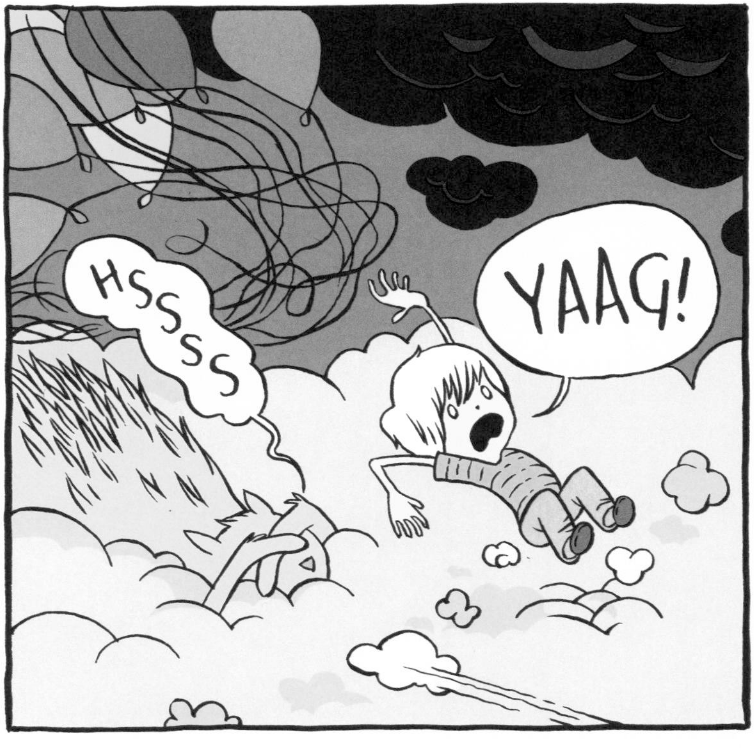
HSSSSS
YAAG!

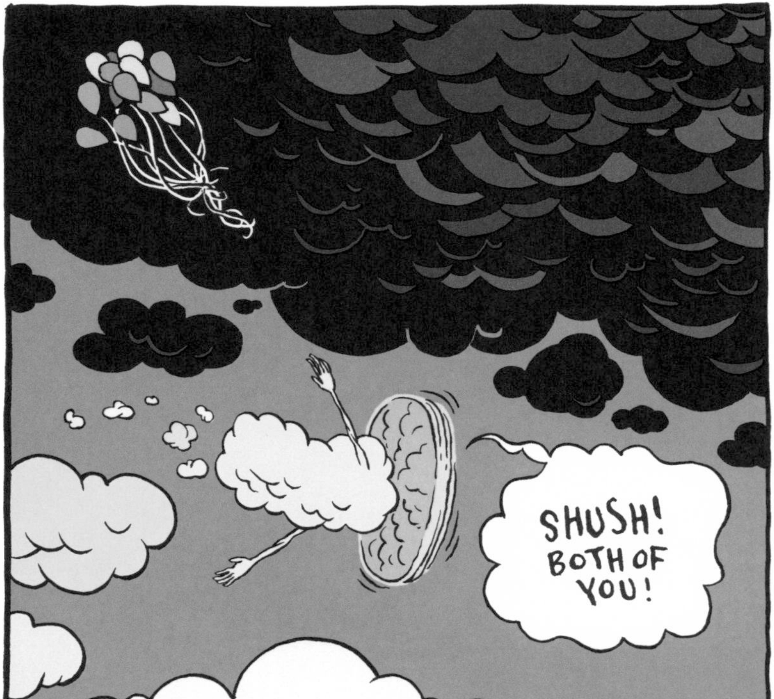
SHUSH! BOTH OF YOU!

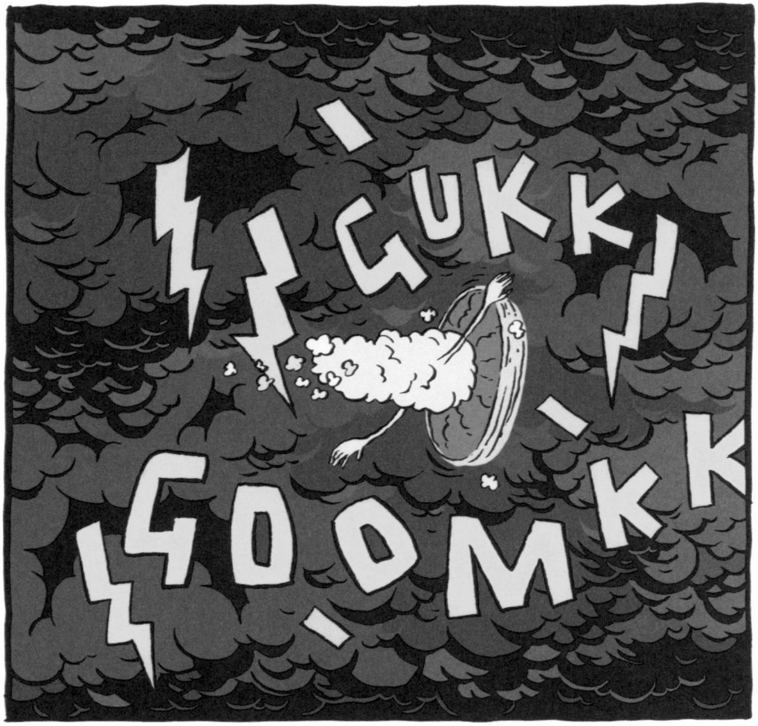
GUKK
GOOMKK

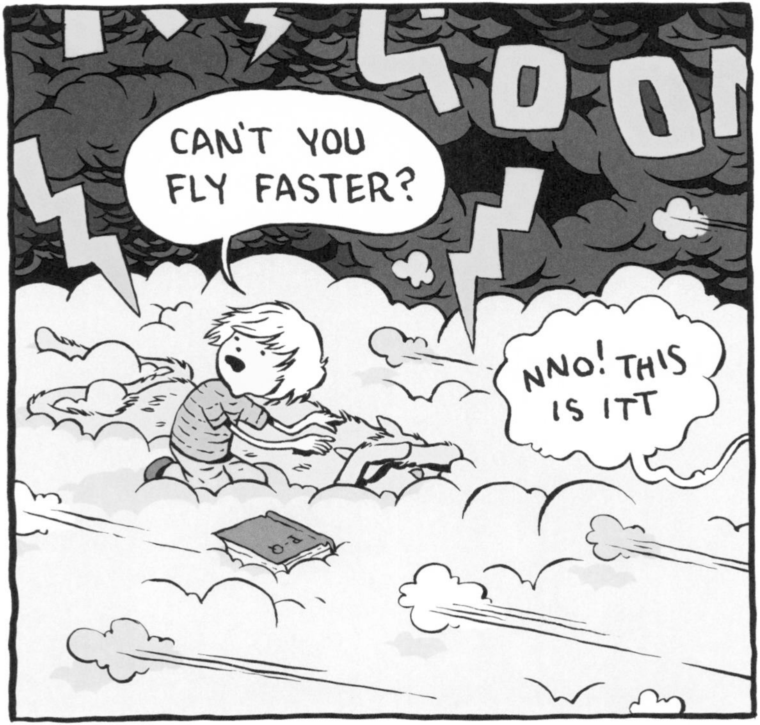
CAN'T YOU FLY FASTER?
NNO! THIS IS ITT

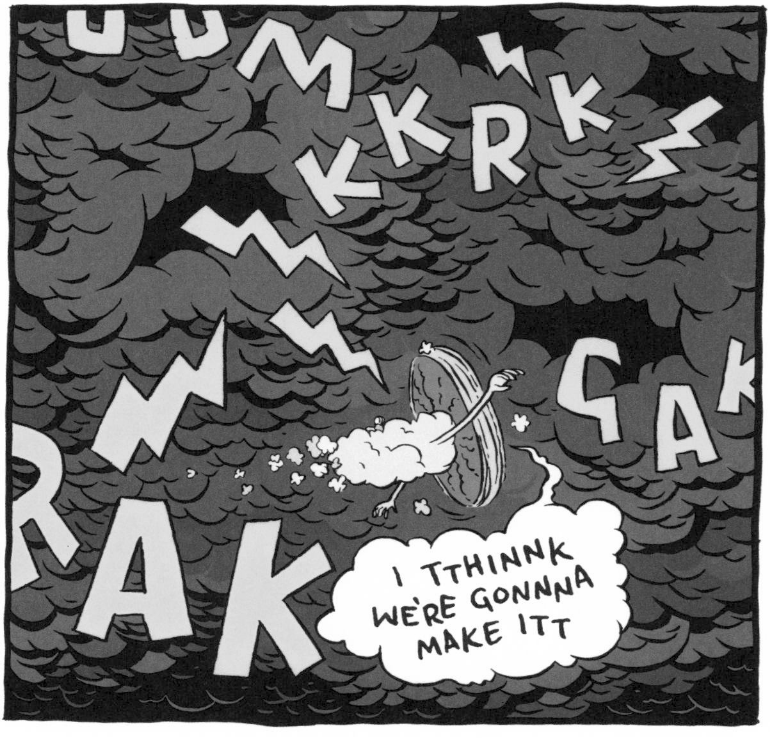
KKRK
RAK
I TTHINNK WE'RE GONNNA MAKE ITT

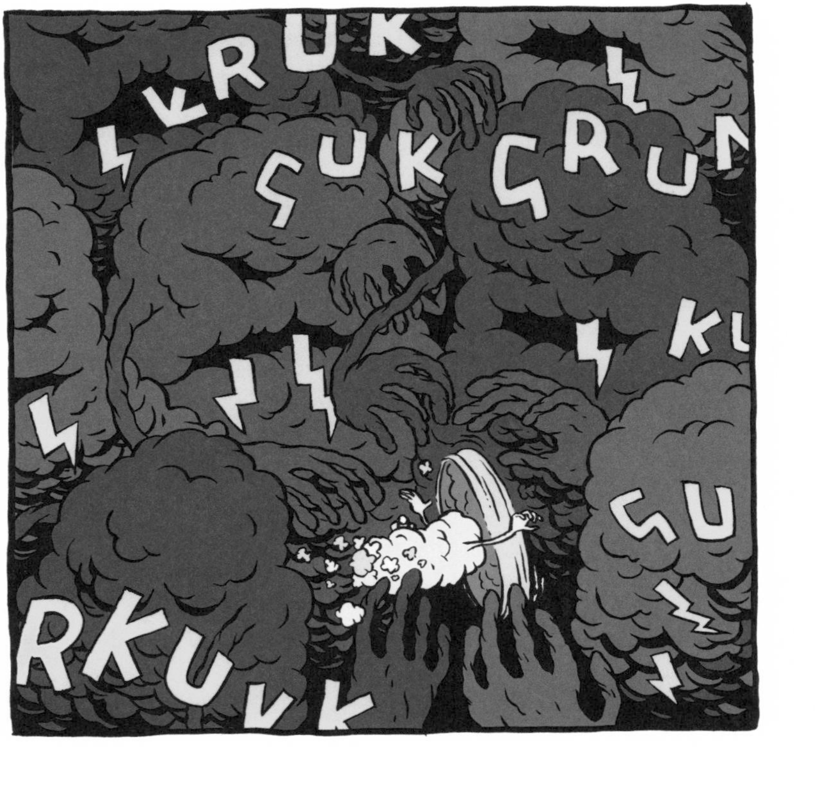
KRUK
UK
RU
KU
U
RKU

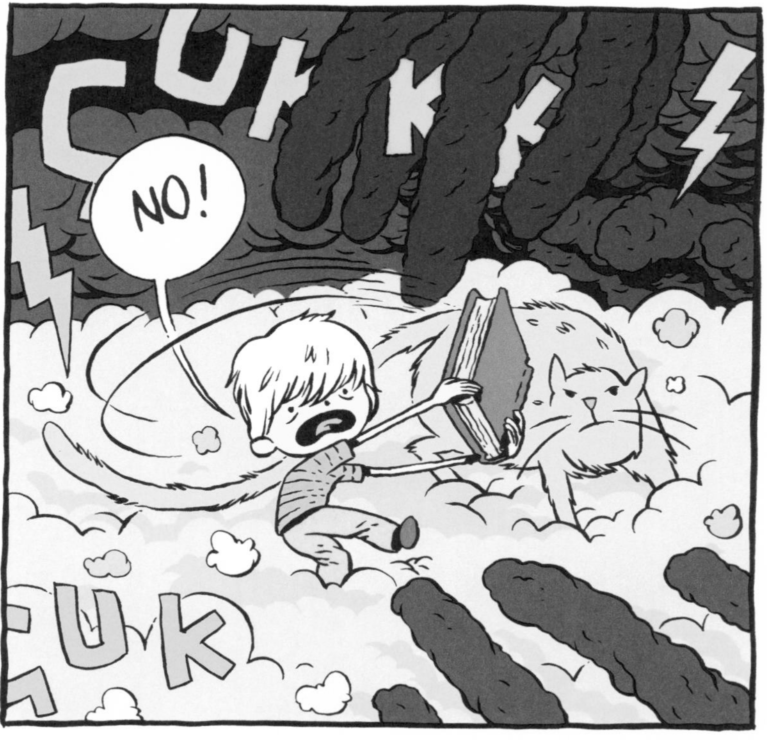
NO!

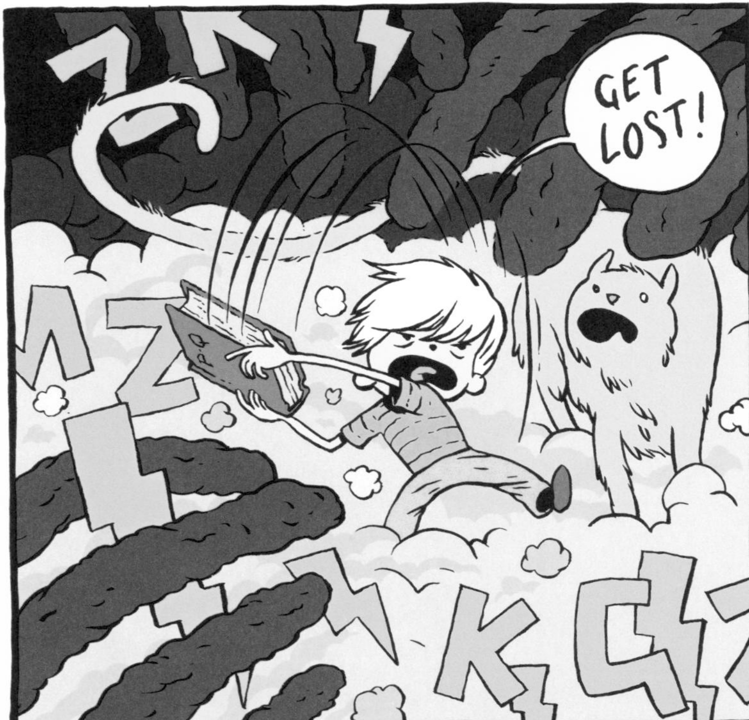
GET LOST!

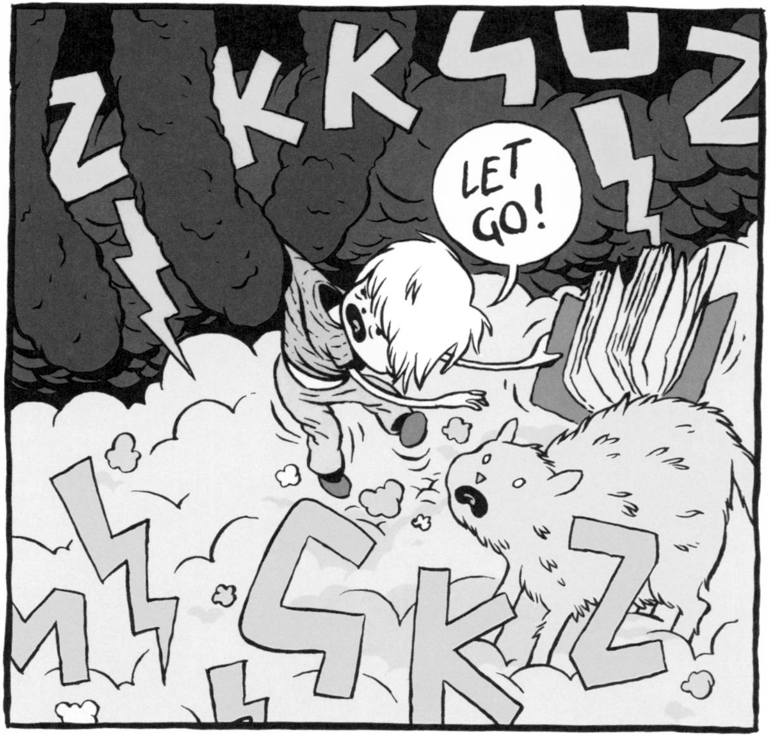
LET GO!

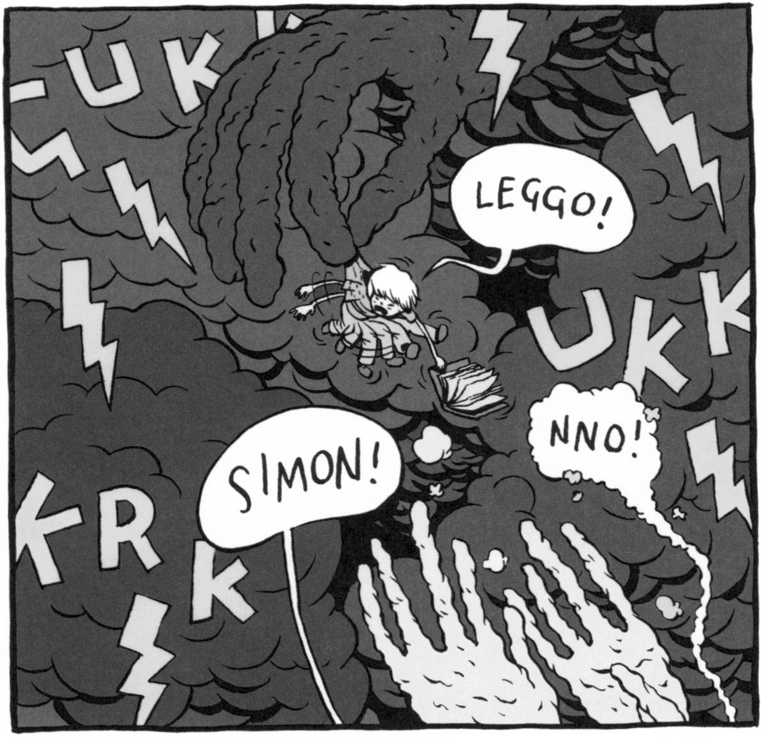
LEGGO!
UKK
SIMON!
NNO!
KRK

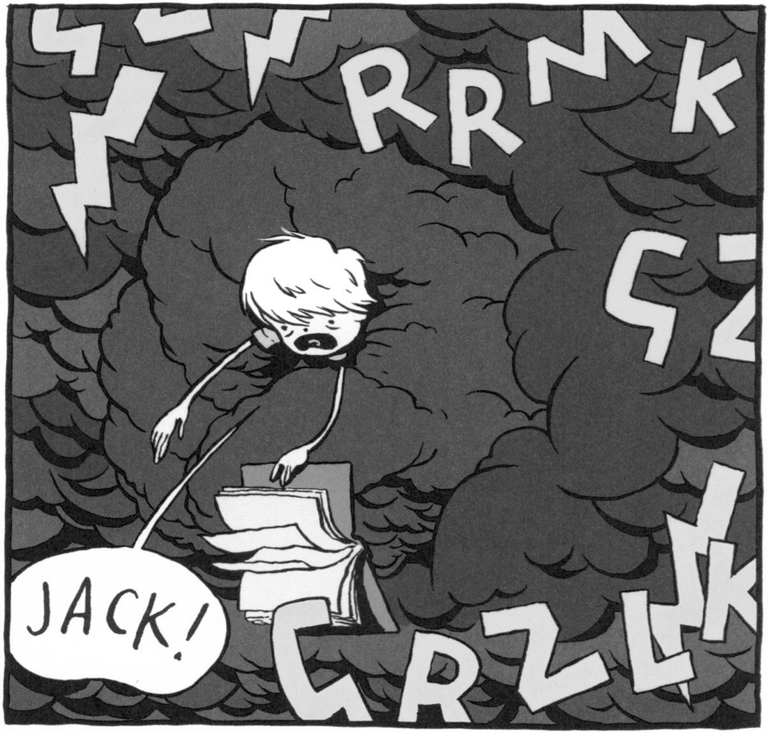
RRMK
JACK!
GRZLK

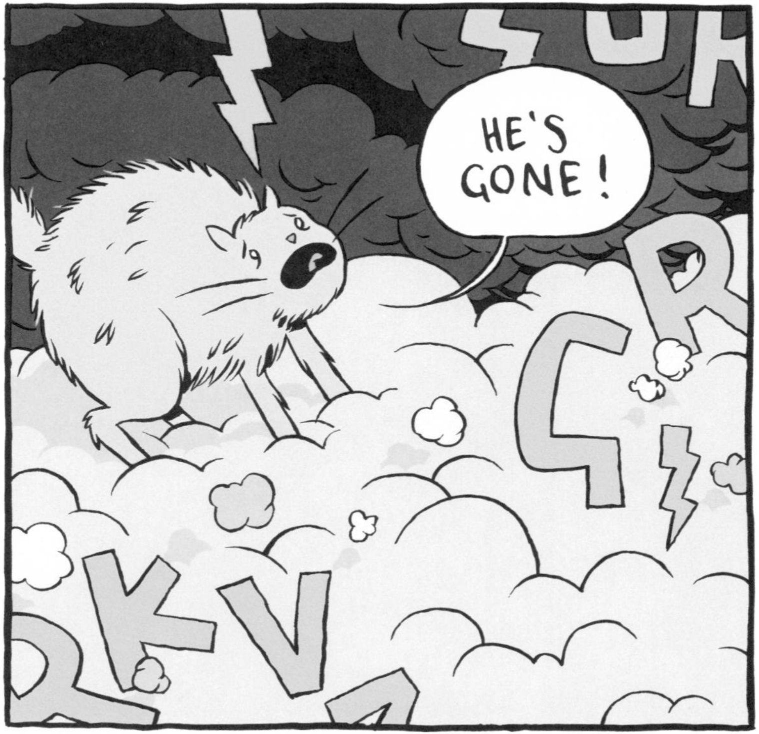
HE'S GONE!

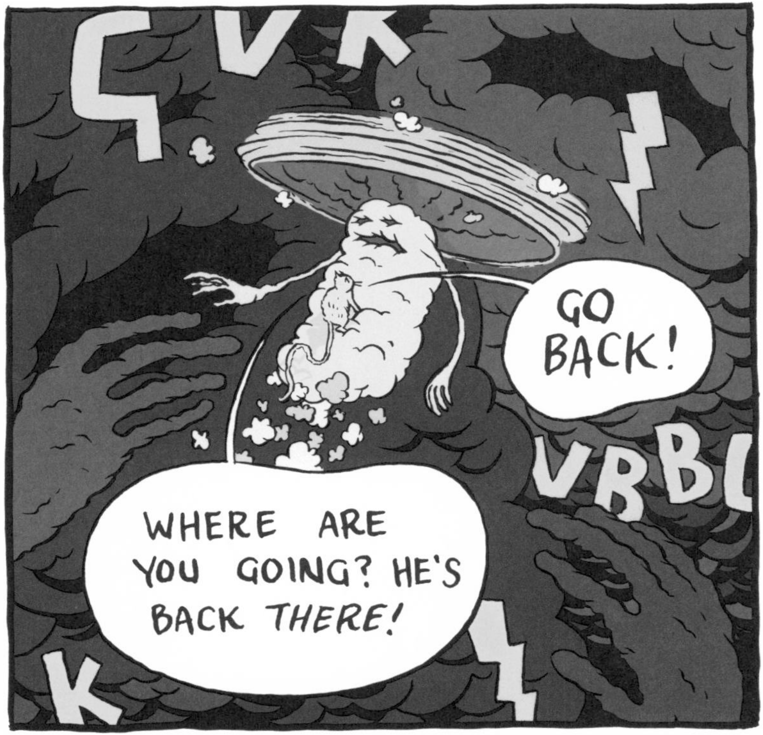
GO BACK!
WHERE ARE YOU GOING? HE'S BACK THERE!

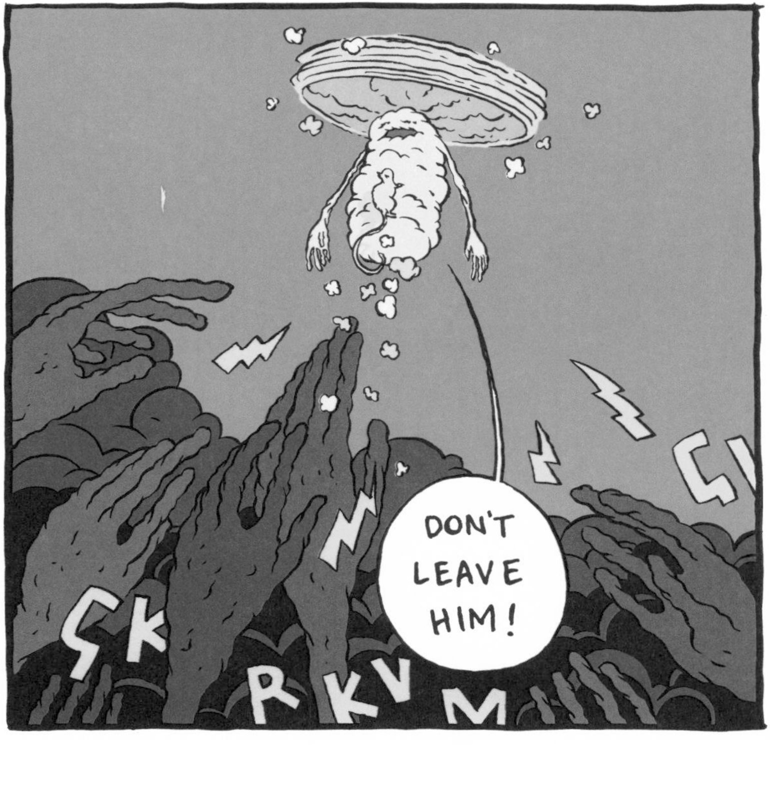
DON'T LEAVE HIM!
SK
RKVM

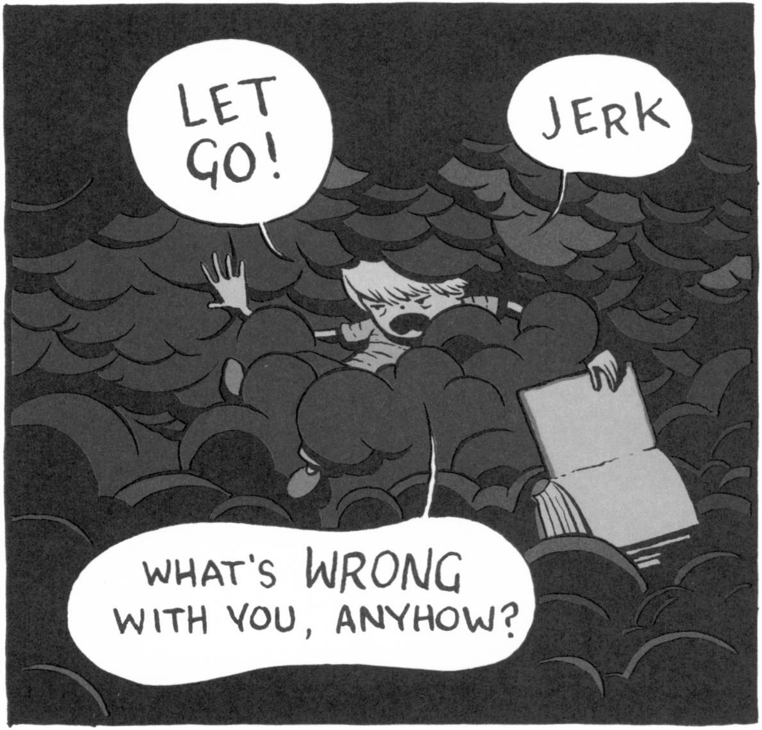
LET GO!
JERK
WHAT'S WRONG WITH YOU, ANYHOW?

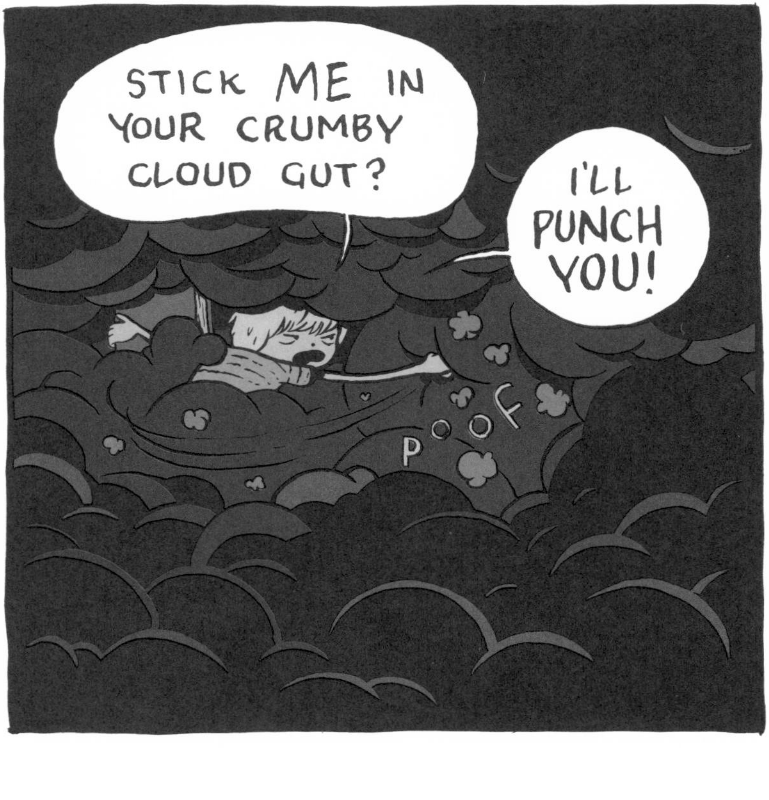
STICK ME IN YOUR CRUMBY CLOUD GUT?
I'LL PUNCH YOU!
POOF

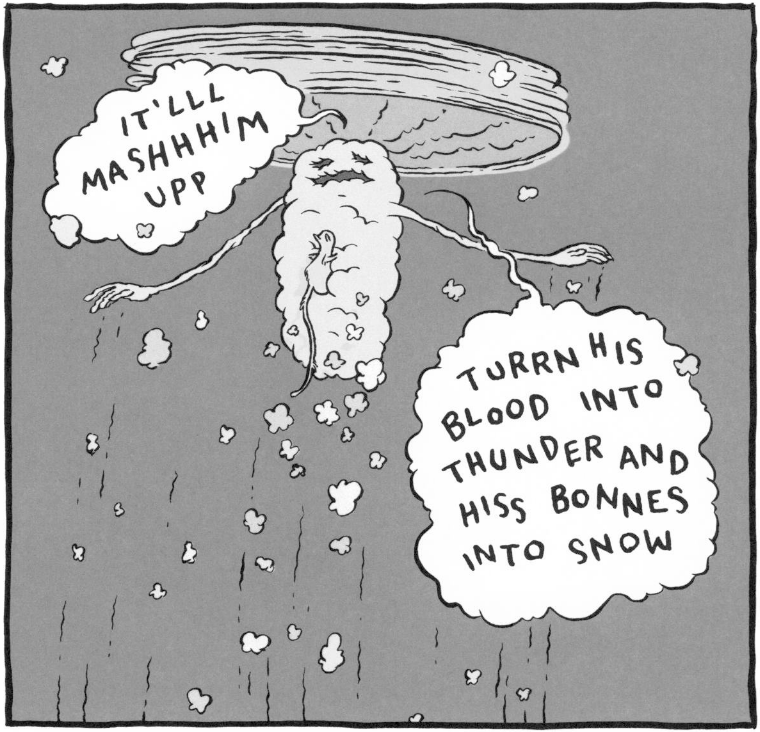
IT'LLL MASHHHIM UPP
TURRN HIS BLOOD INTO THUNDER AND HISS BONNES INTO SNOW

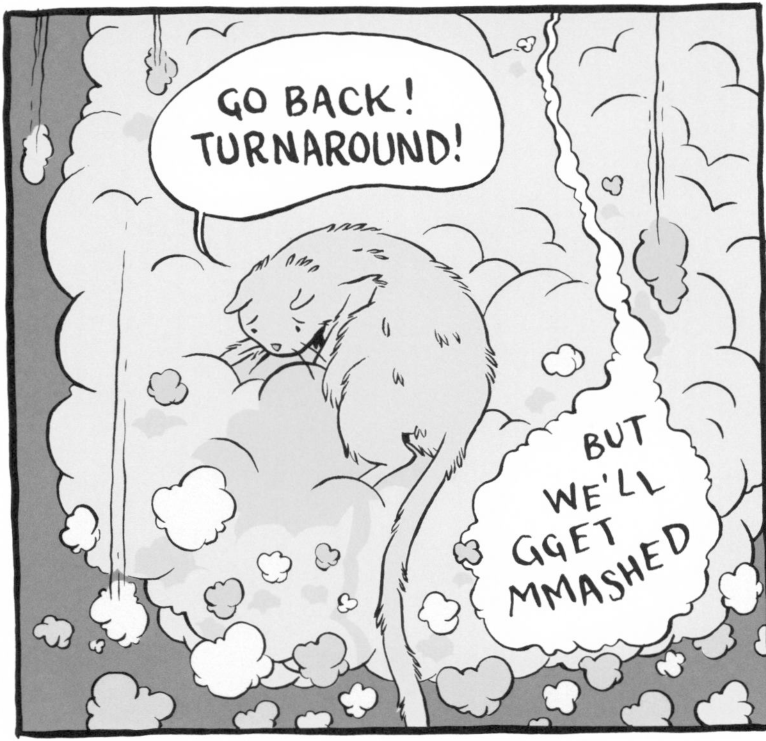
GO BACK! TURNAROUND!
BUT WE'LL GGET MMASHED

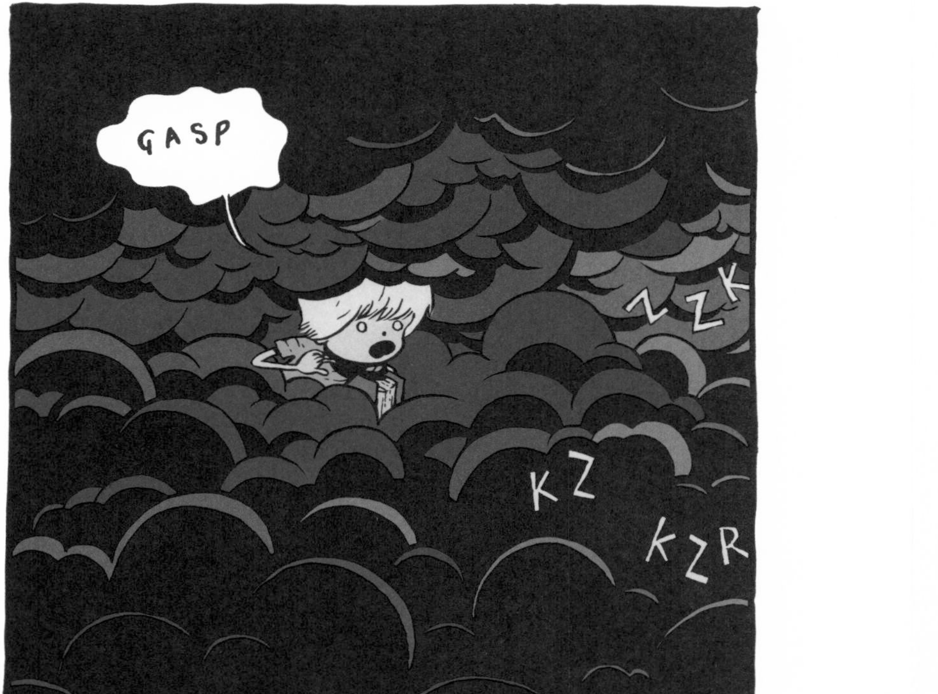
GASP
ZZK
KZ
KZR

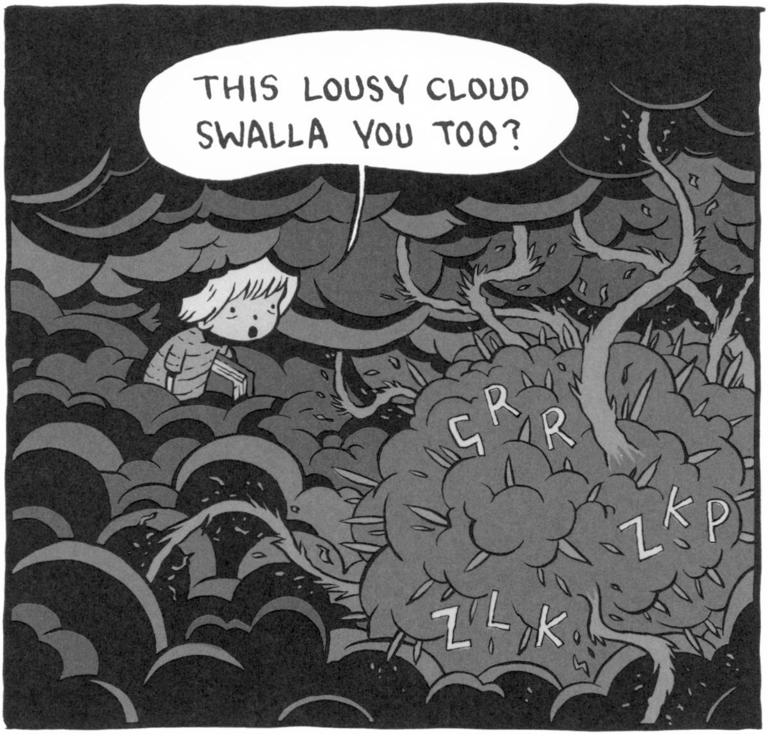
THIS LOUSY CLOUD SWALLA YOU TOO?
GRR
ZKP
ZLK

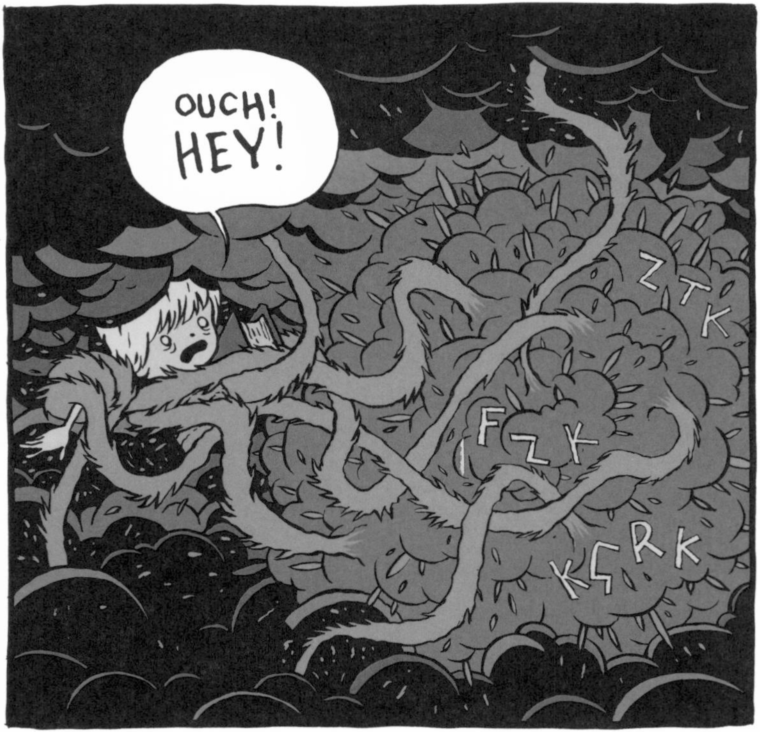
OUCH! HEY!
ZTK
FZK
KSRK

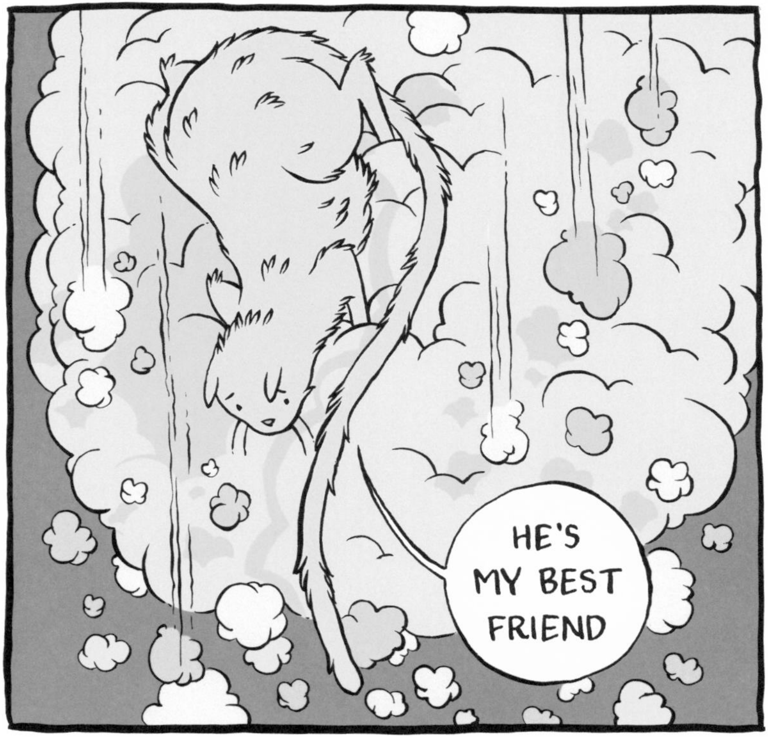
HE'S MY BEST FRIEND

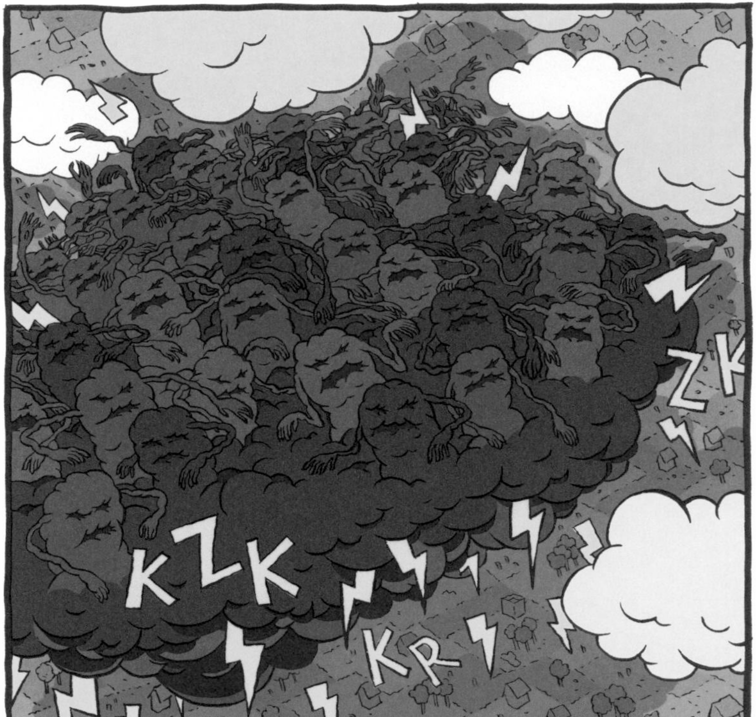
ZK
KZK
KR

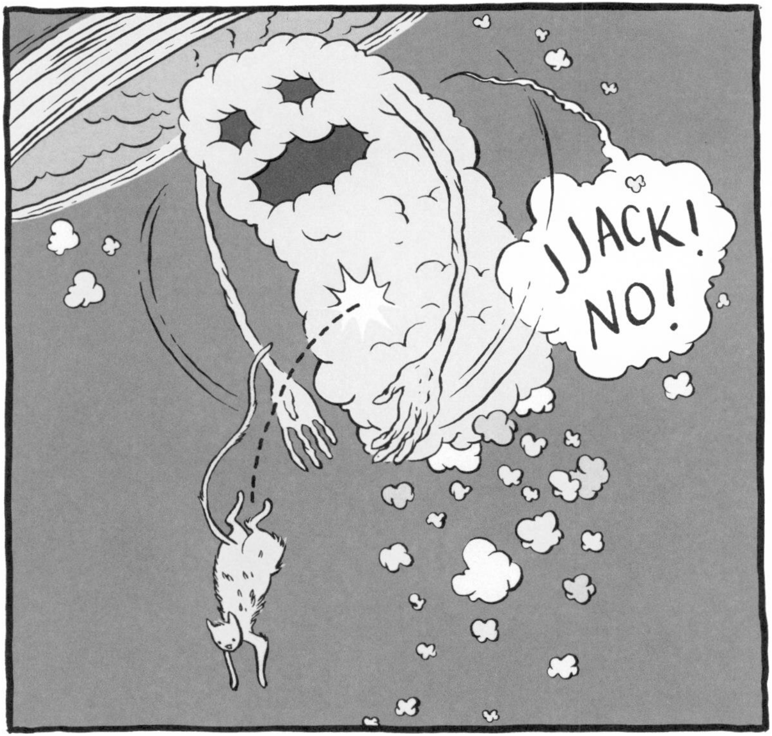
JACK! NO!

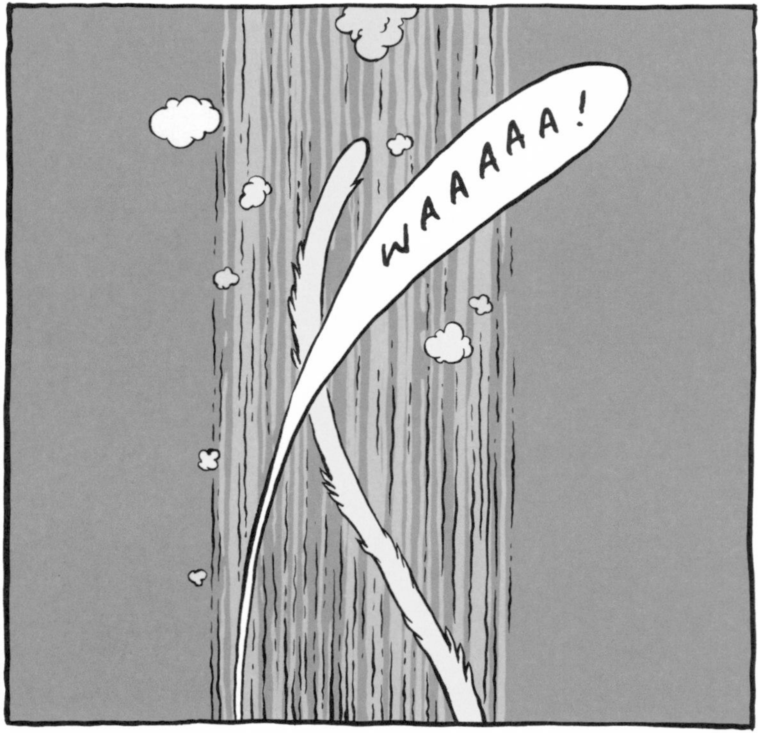
WAAAAAA!

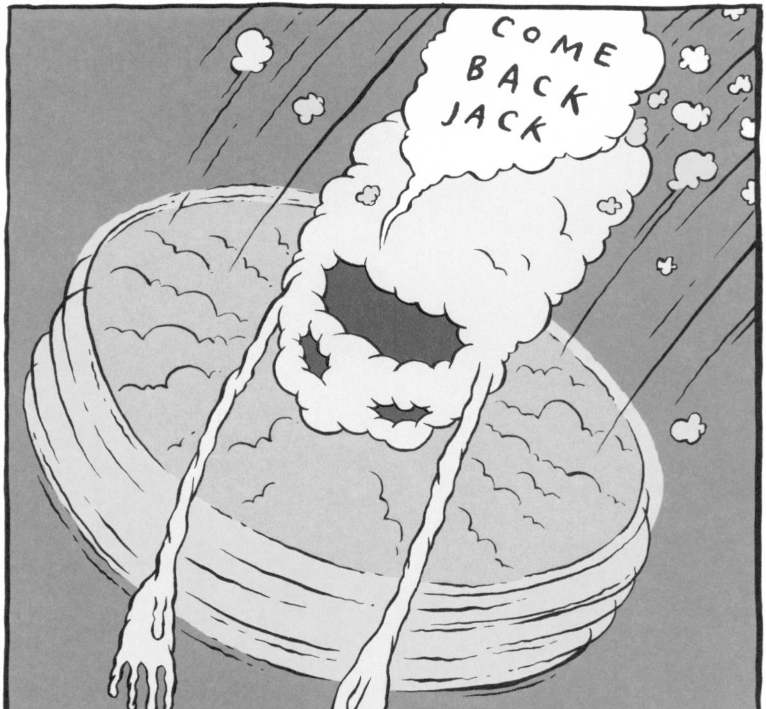
COME BACK JACK

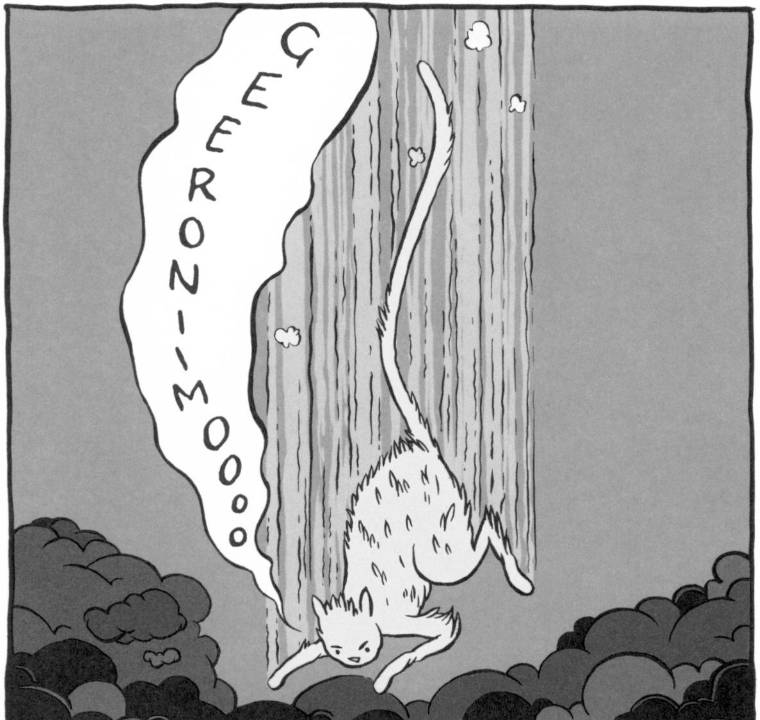
GEERONIIMOOooo

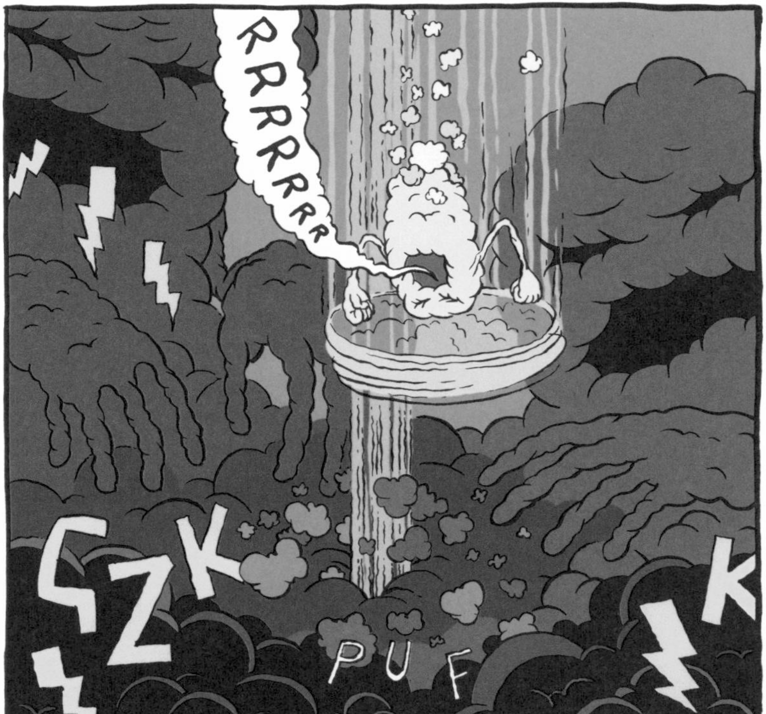
RRRRRRRRRR
CZK
PUF
K

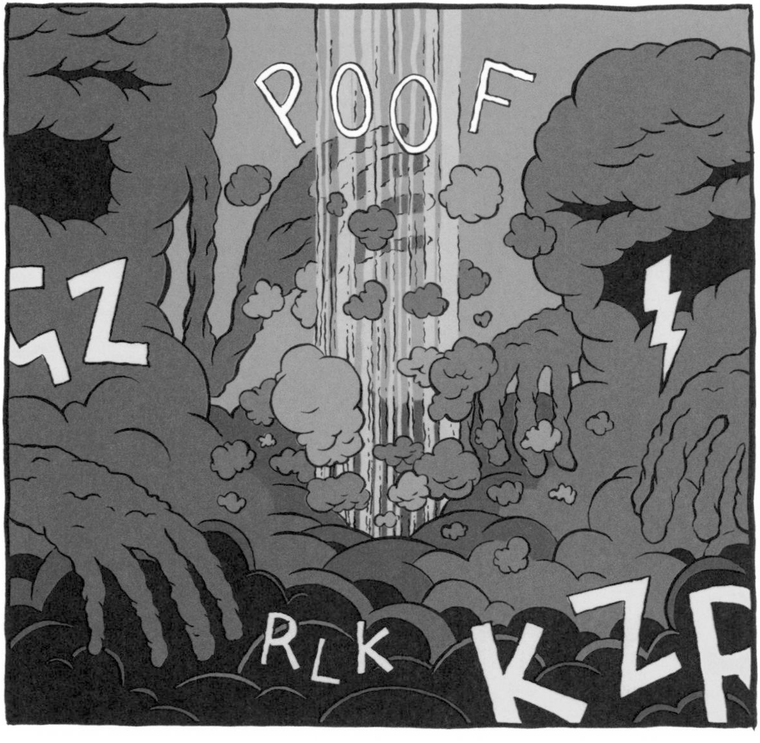
POOF
RLK

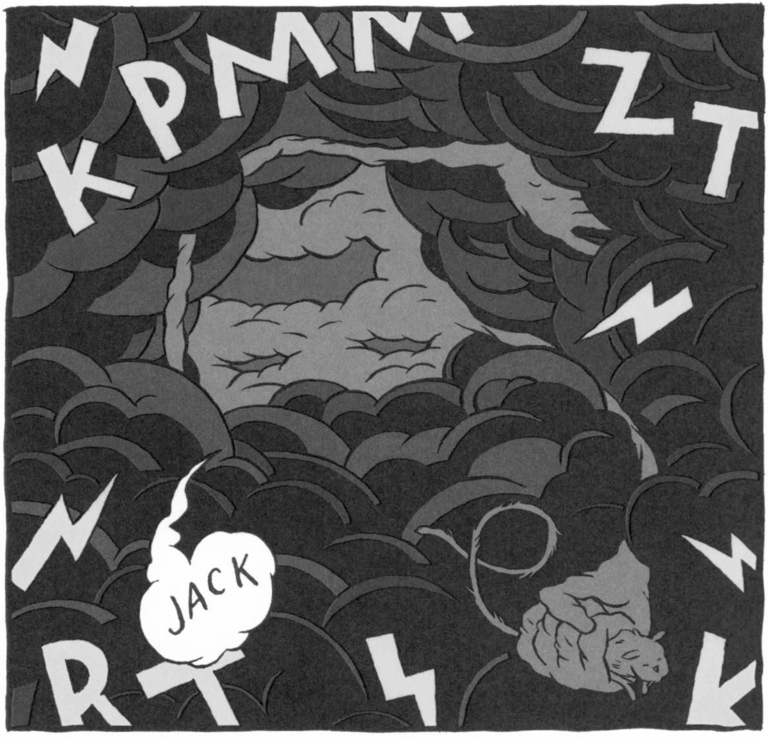
JACK

ZK
KZ
ZL
KL
KR
ZR

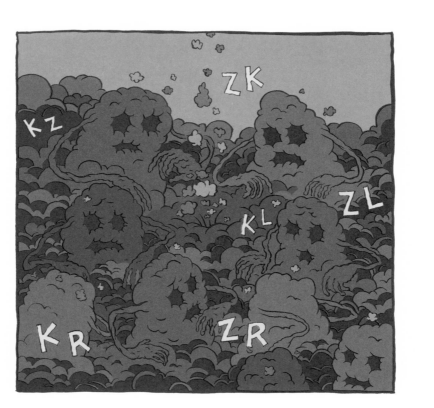

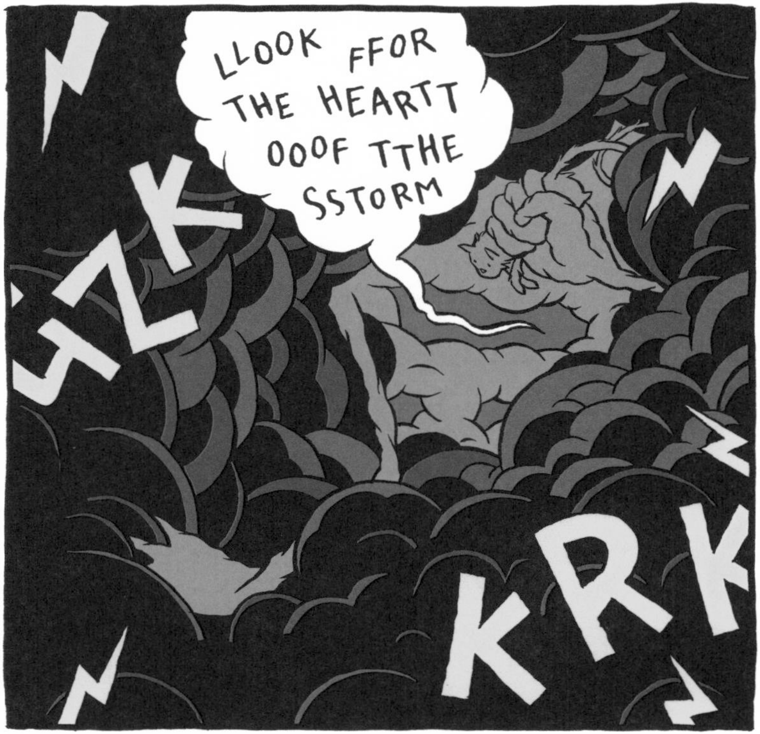
LLOOK FFOR THE HEARTT OOOF TTHE SSTORM
GZK
KRK

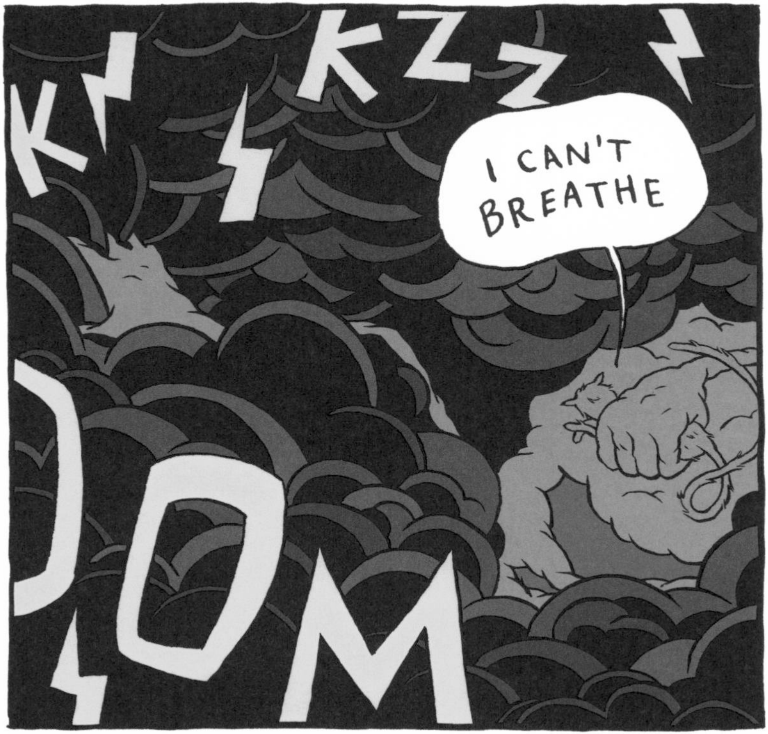
I CAN'T BREATHE

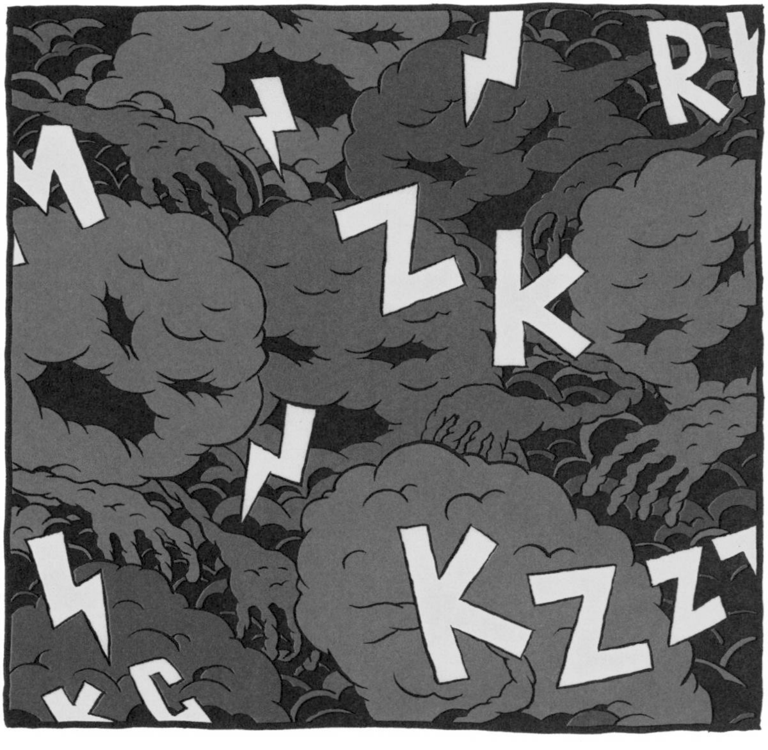
ZK
KZZ

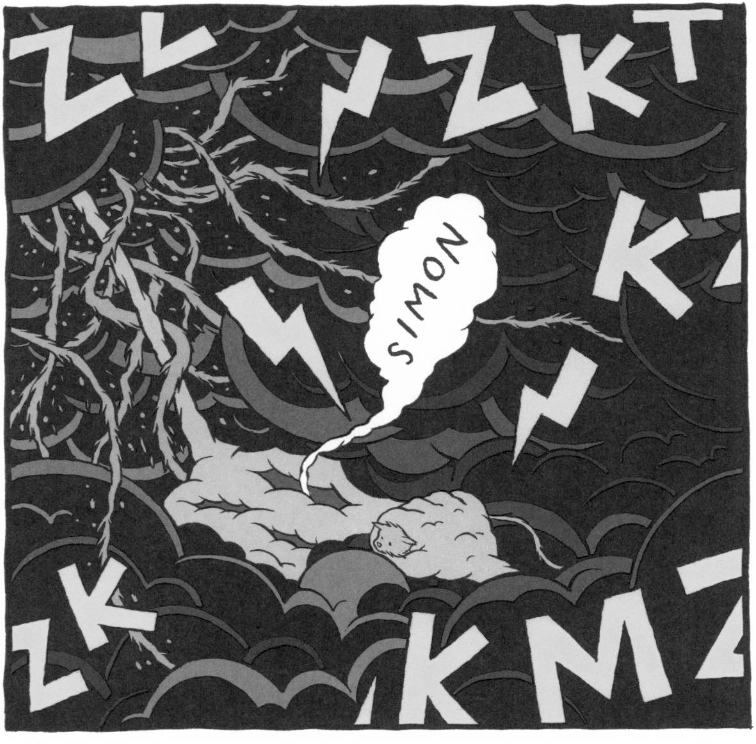
SIMON

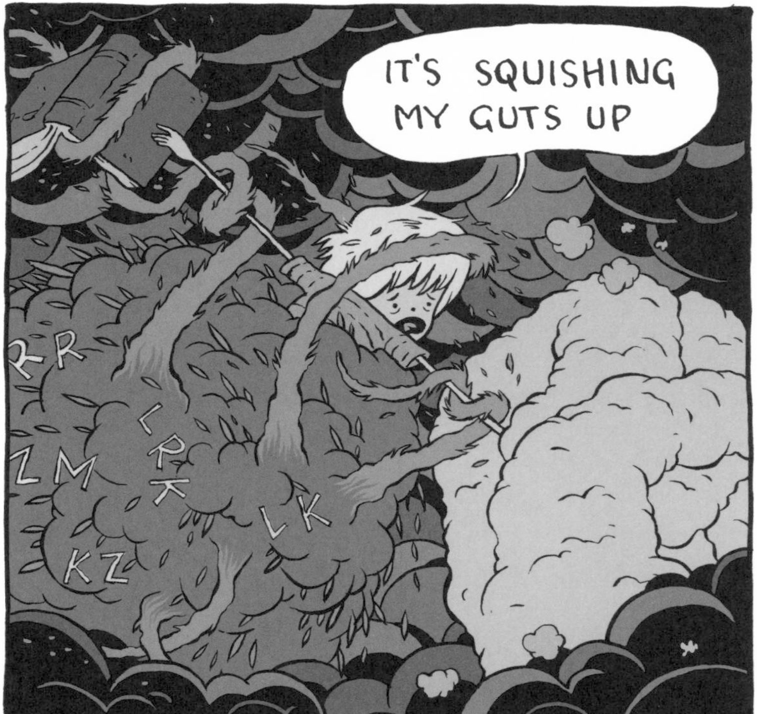
IT'S SQUISHING MY GUTS UP
RR
LRK
ZM
LK
KZ

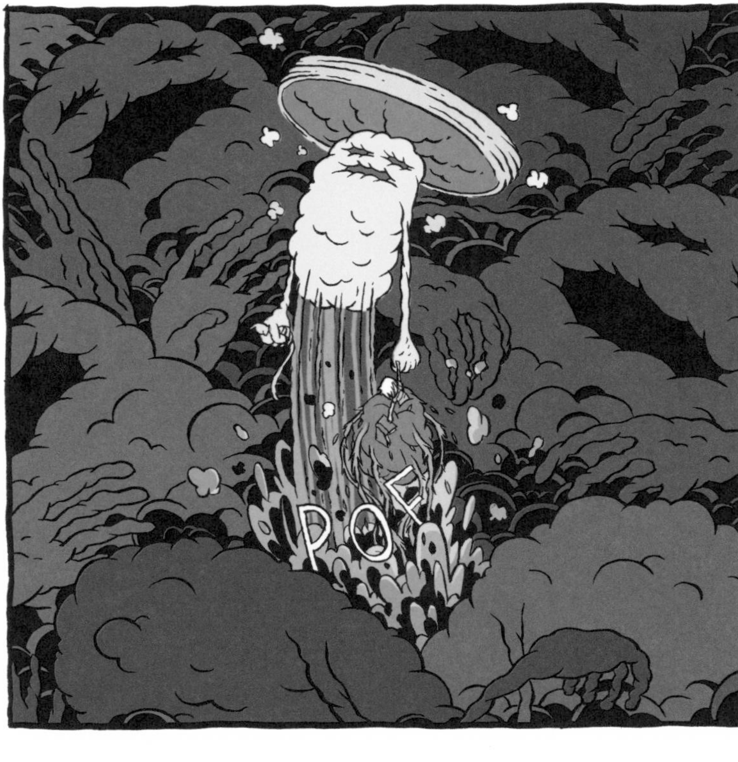
POF

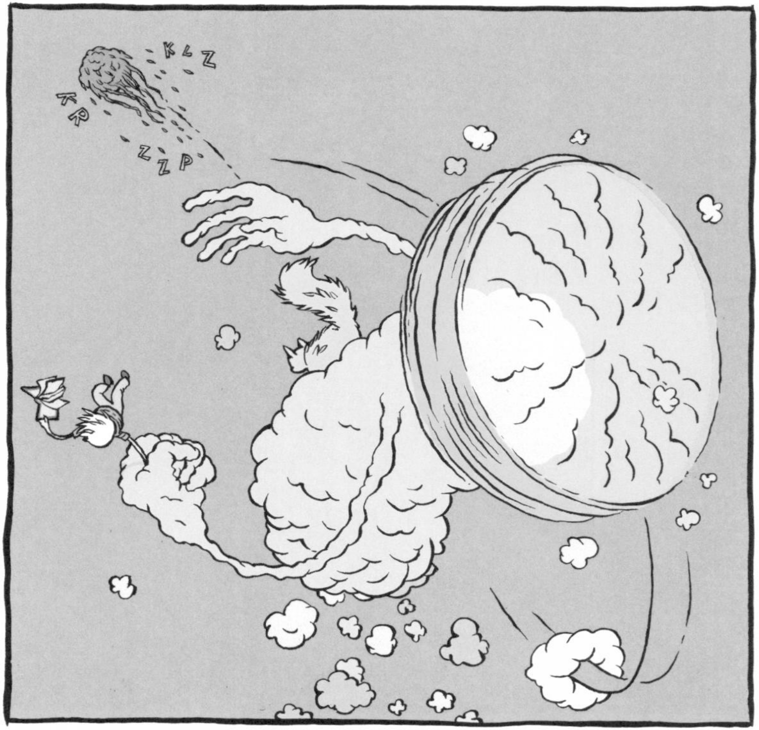
KRZZP
KLZ

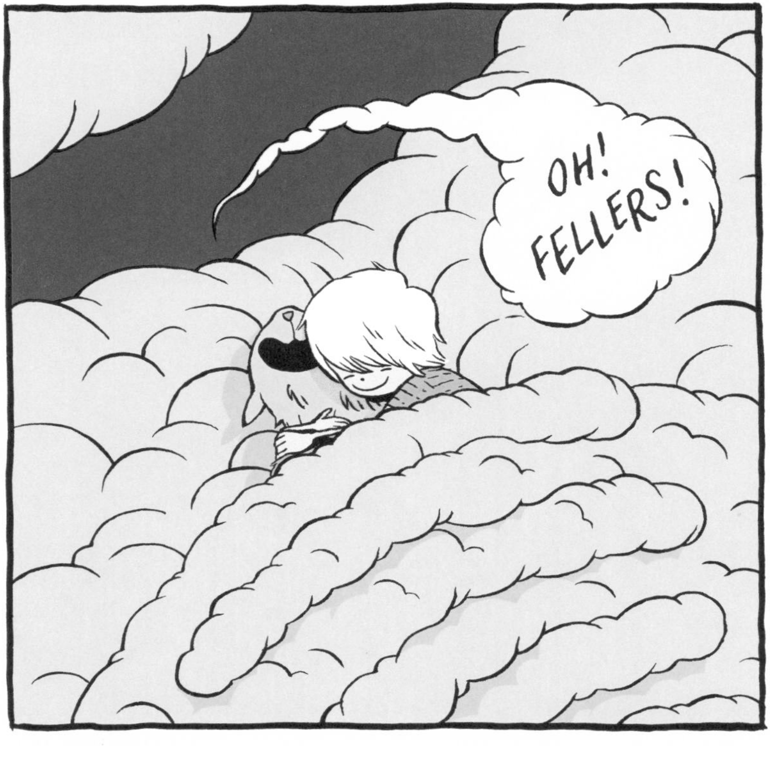
OH! FELLERS!

K
R
Z
L!
Z
L
K
K
R

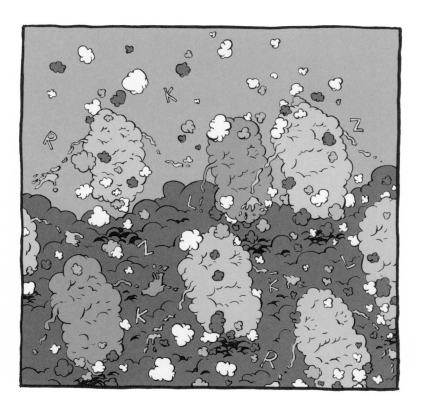

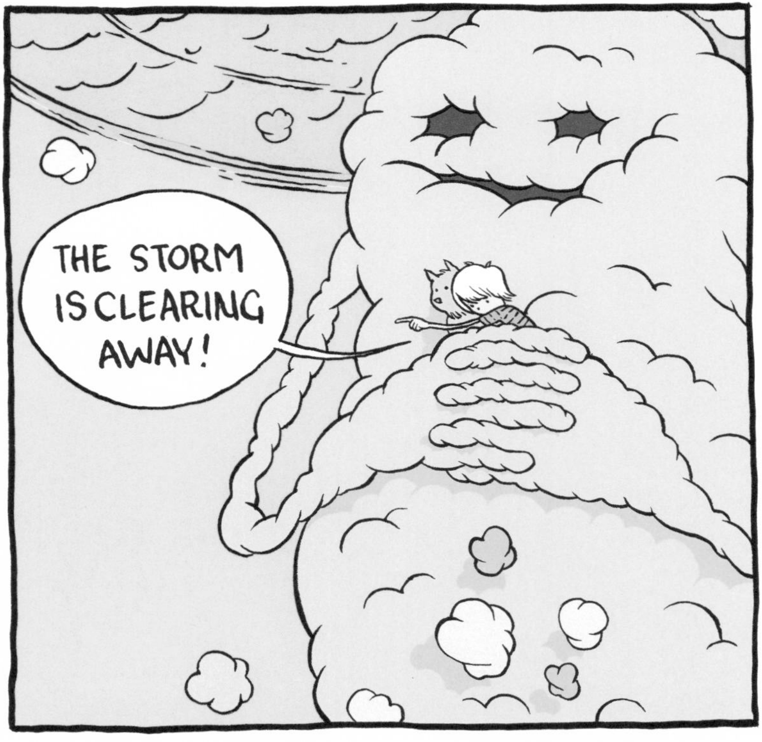
THE STORM IS CLEARING AWAY!

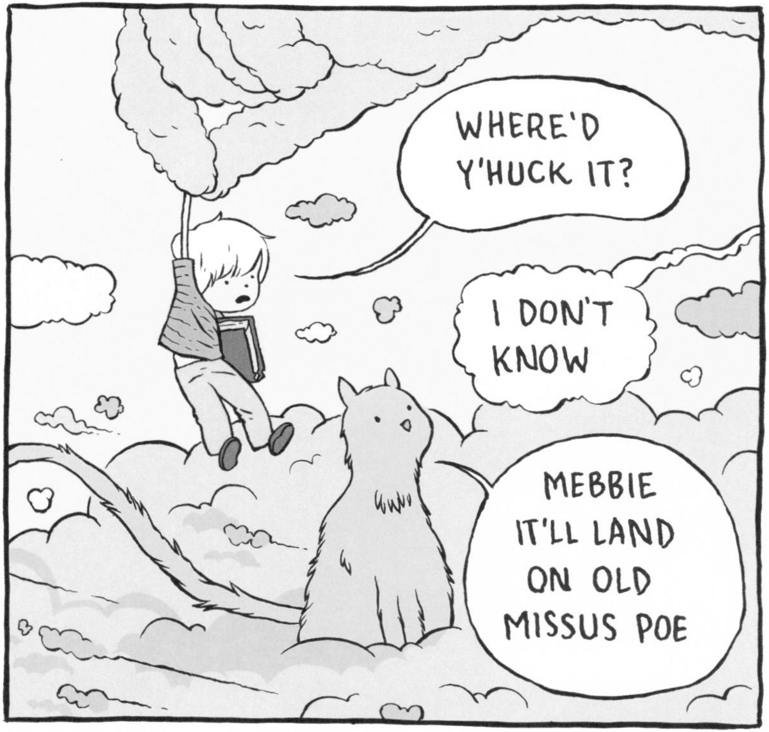
WHERE'D Y'HUCK IT?
I DON'T KNOW
MEBBIE IT'LL LAND ON OLD MISSUS POE

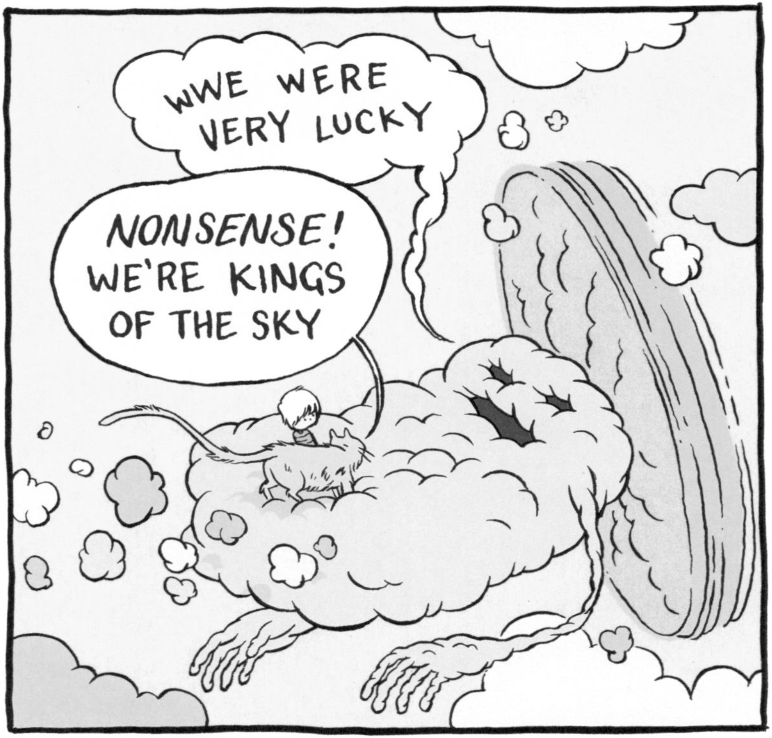
WWE WERE VERY LUCKY
NONSENSE! WE'RE KINGS OF THE SKY

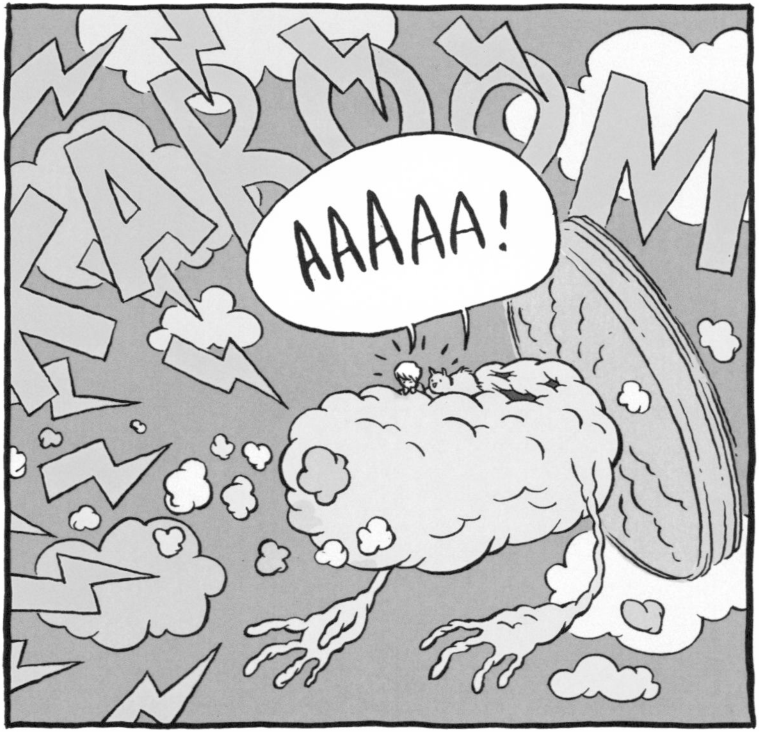
AAAAA!

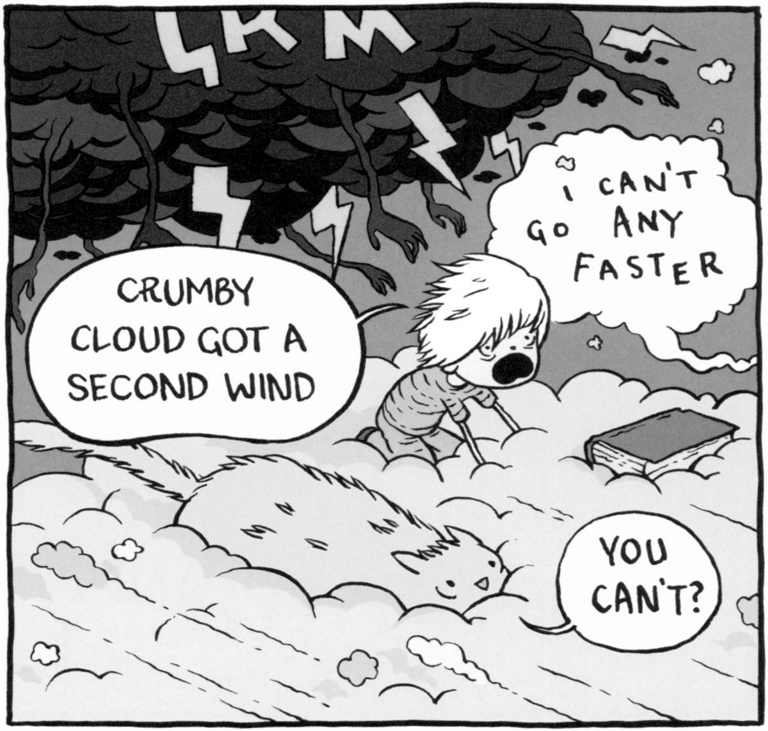
CRM
I CAN'T GO ANY FASTER
CRUMBY CLOUD GOT A SECOND WIND
YOU CAN'T?

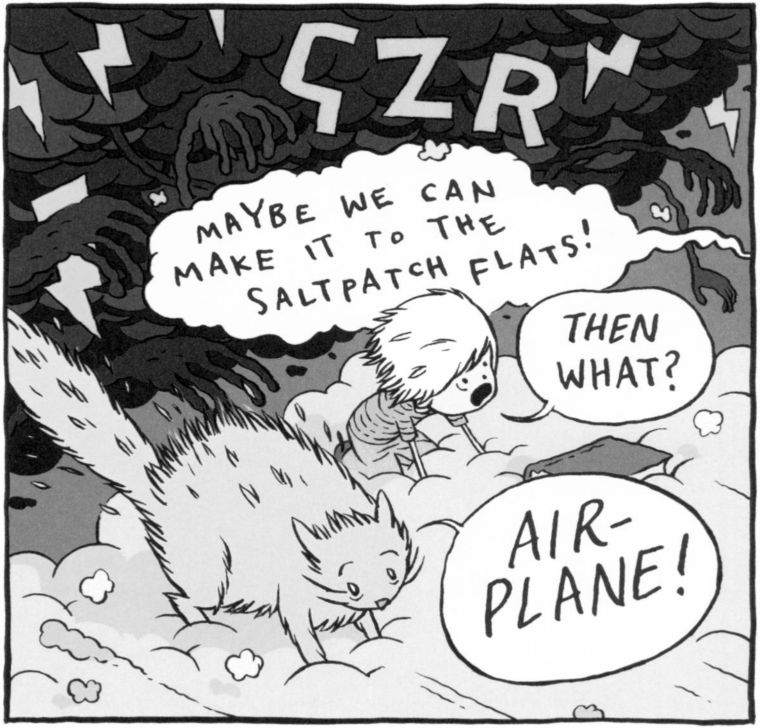
CZR
MAYBE WE CAN MAKE IT TO THE SALTPATCH FLATS!
THEN WHAT?
AIR-PLANE!

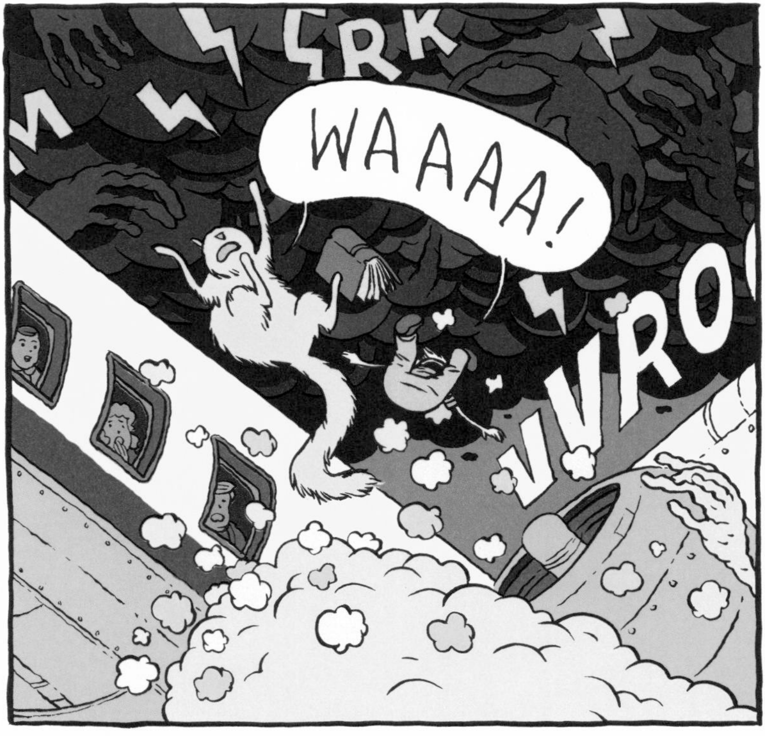
CRK
WAAAA!
VVRO

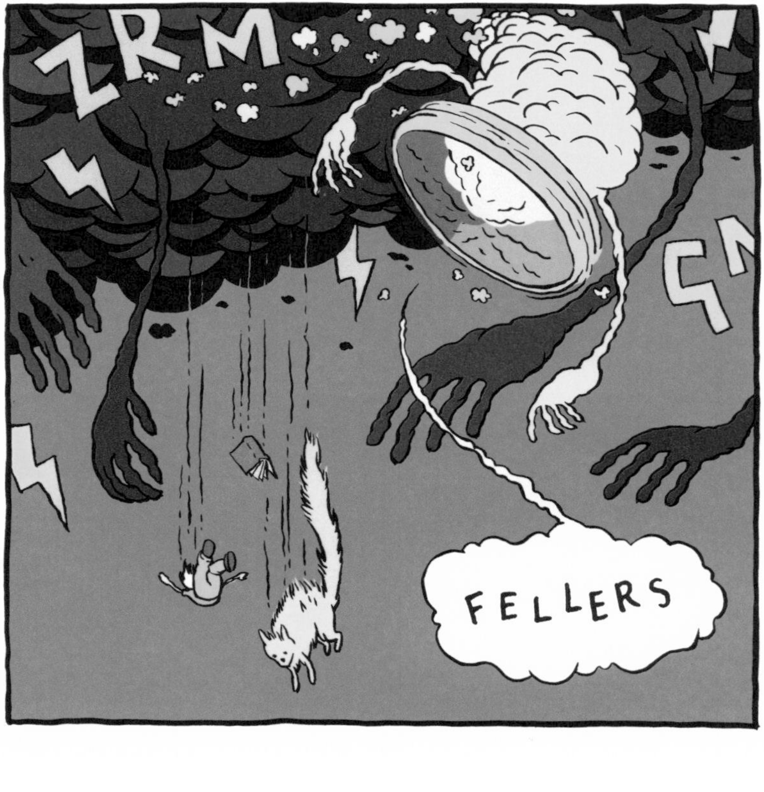
ZRM
FELLERS

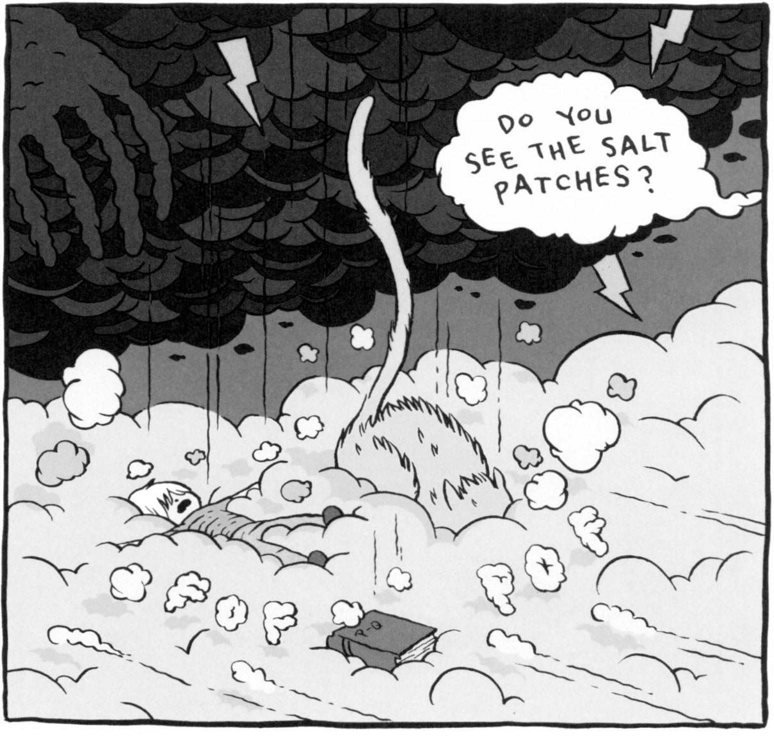
DO YOU SEE THE SALT PATCHES?

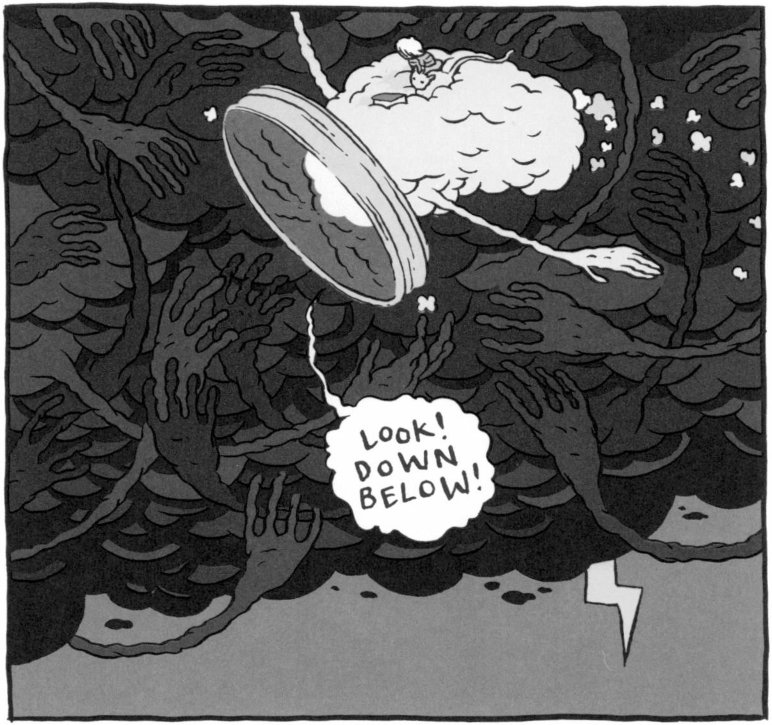
LOOK! DOWN BELOW!

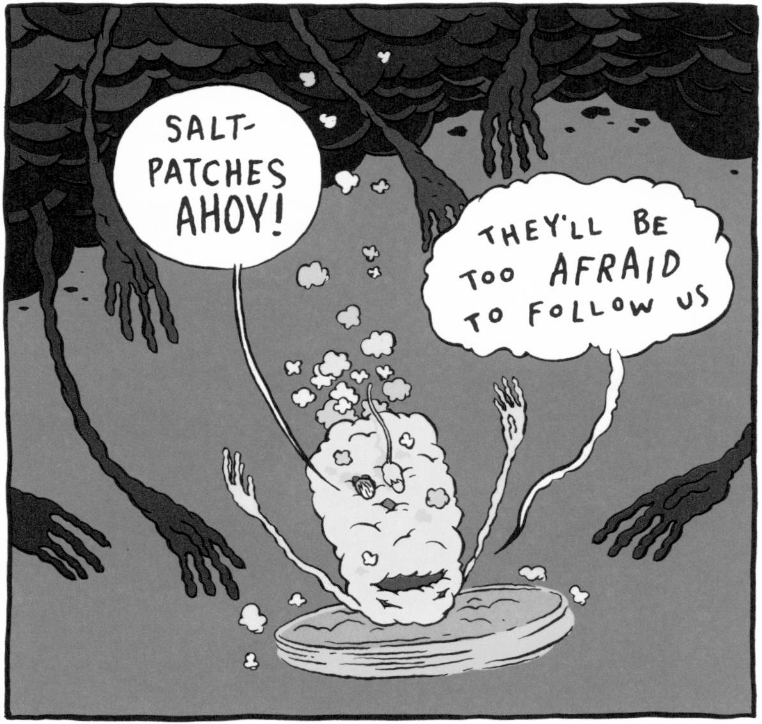
SALT-PATCHES AHOY!
THEY'LL BE TOO AFRAID TO FOLLOW US

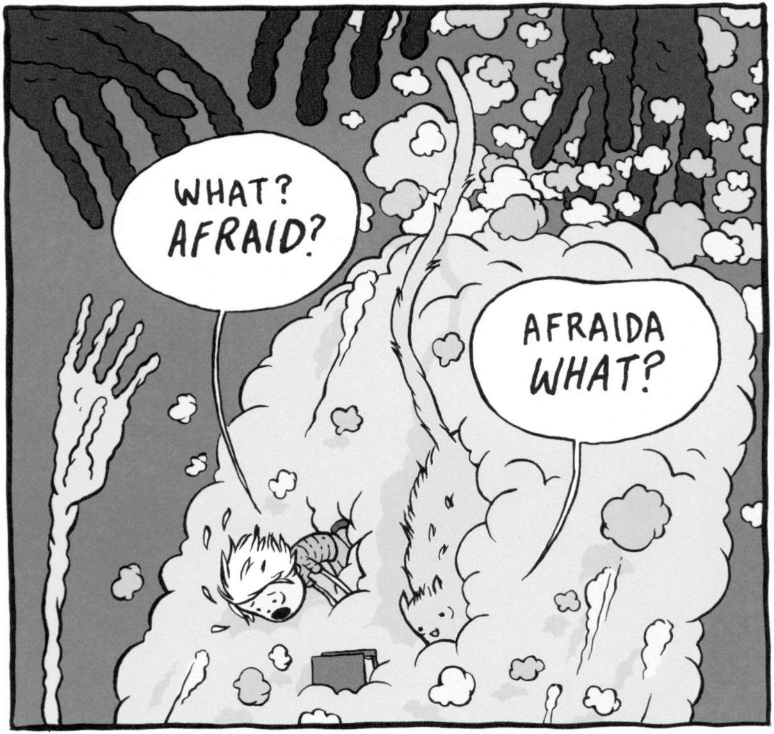
WHAT? AFRAID?
AFRAIDA WHAT?

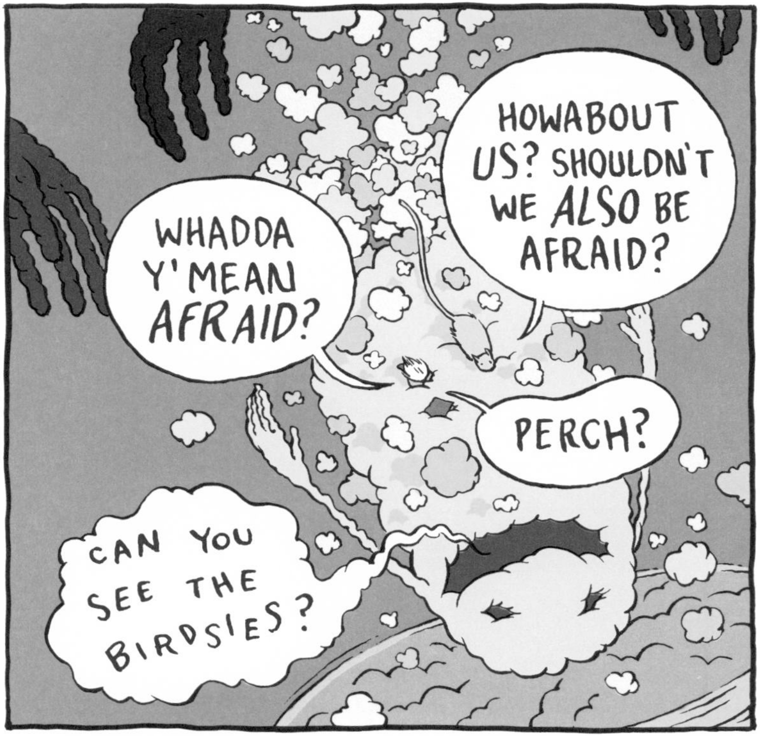
WHADDA Y'MEAN AFRAID?
HOWABOUT US? SHOULDN'T WE ALSO BE AFRAID?
PERCH?
CAN YOU SEE THE BIRDSIES?

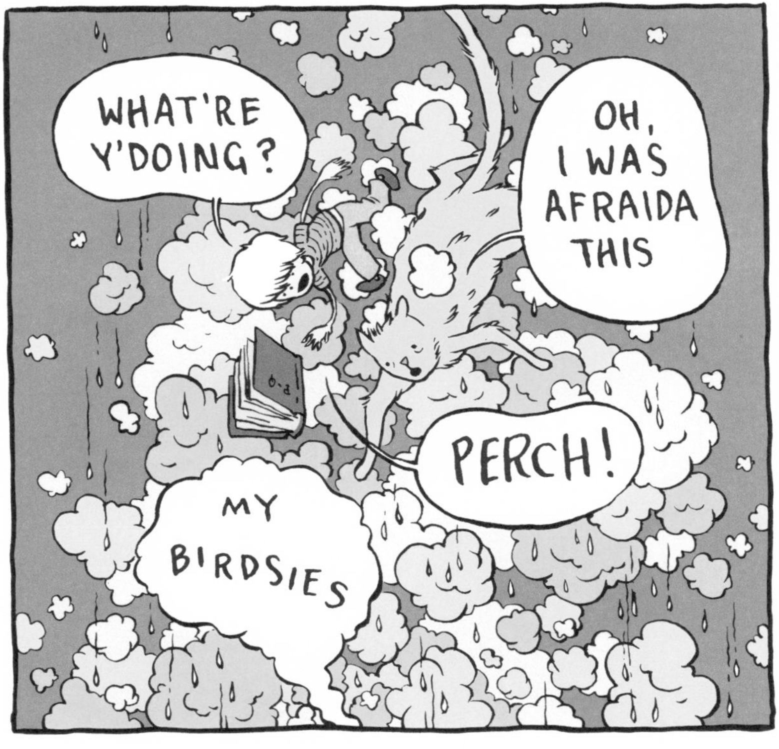
WHAT'RE Y'DOING?
OH, I WAS AFRAIDA THIS
PERCH!
MY BIRDSIES

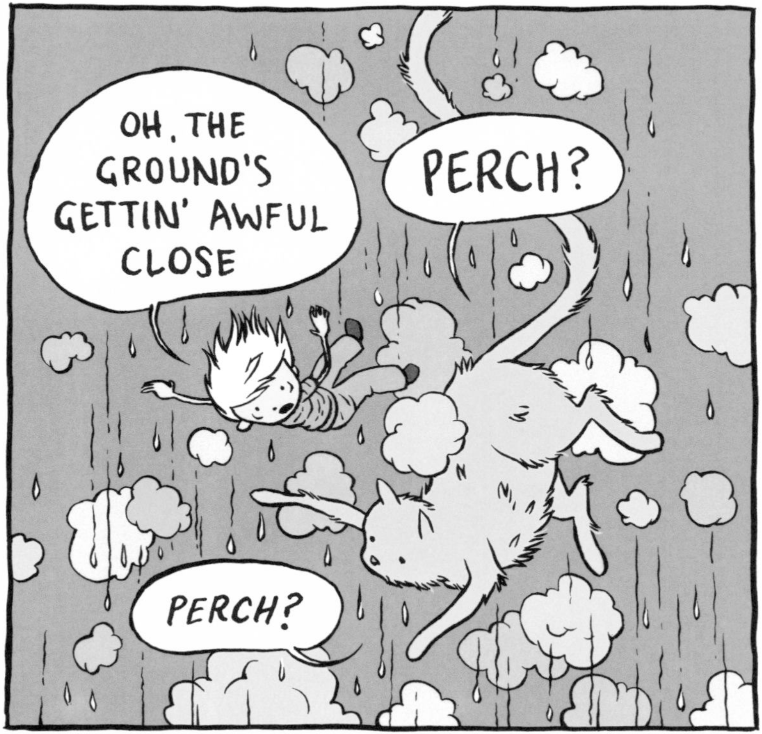
OH, THE GROUND'S GETTIN' AWFUL CLOSE
PERCH?
PERCH?

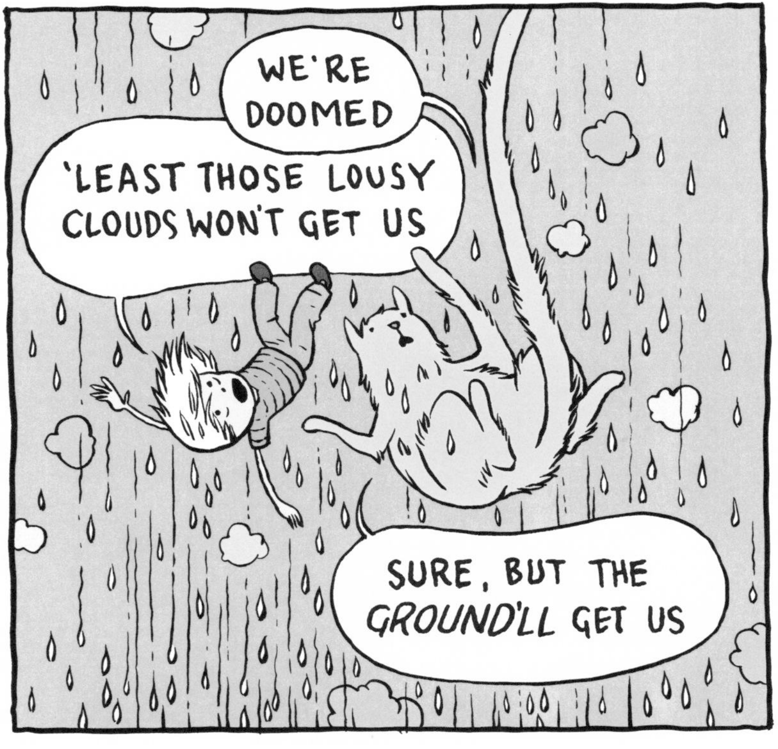
WE'RE DOOMED
'LEAST THOSE LOUSY CLOUDS WON'T GET US
SURE, BUT THE *GROUND'LL* GET US

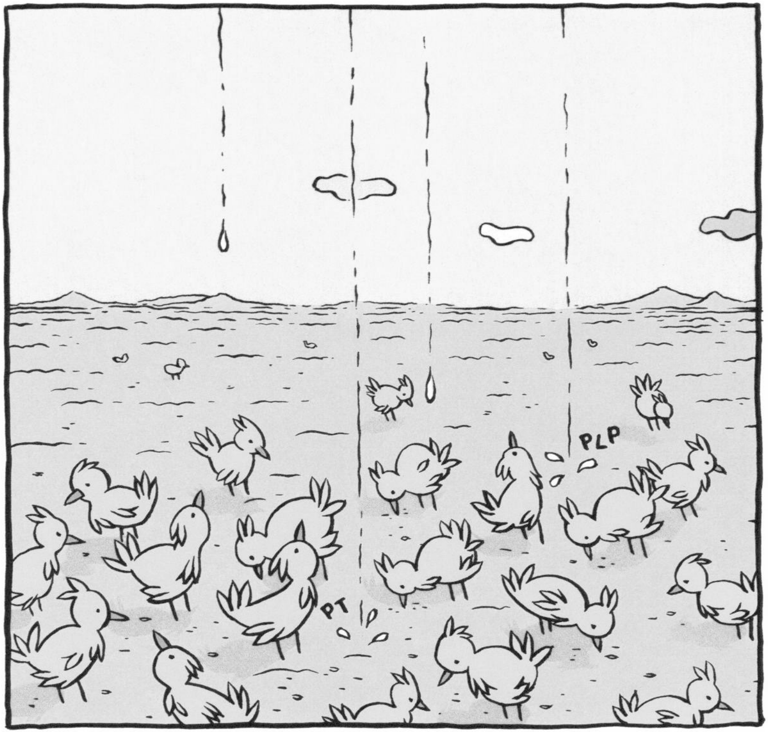
PLP
PT

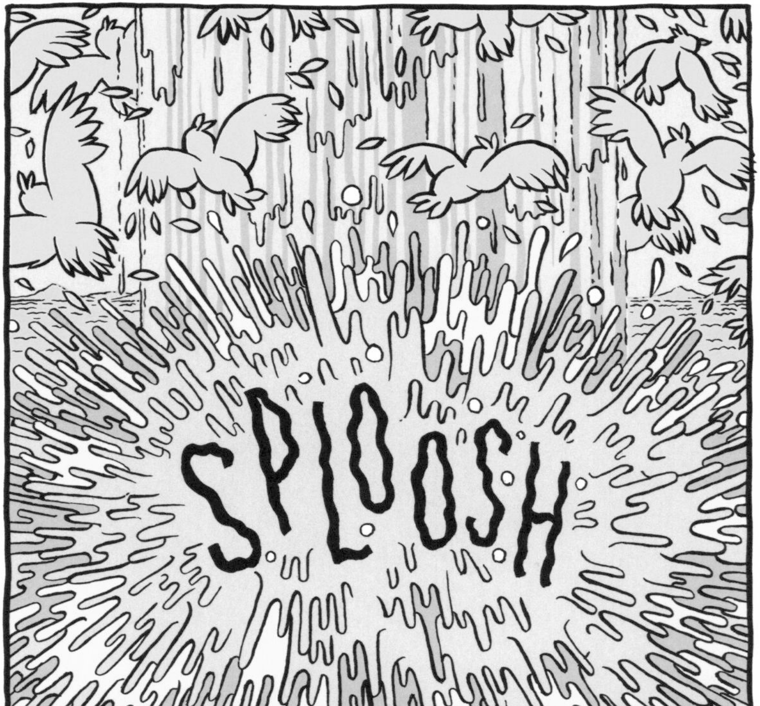
SPLOOSH

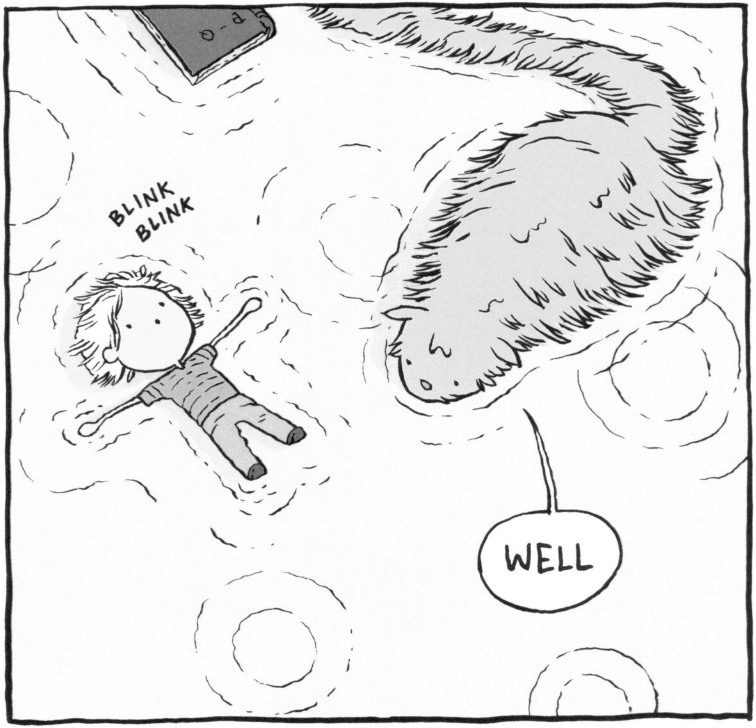
BLINK
BLINK
WELL

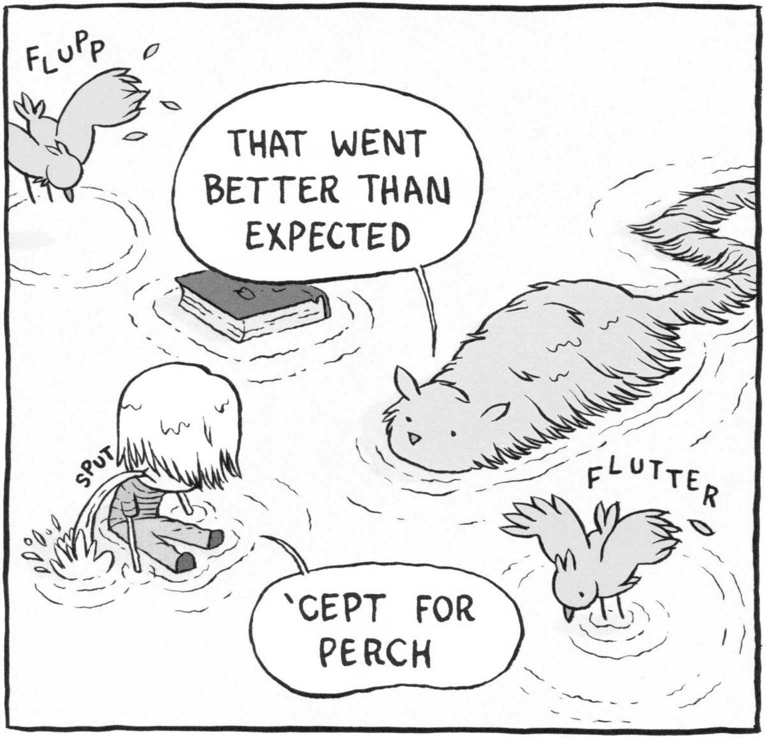
FLUPP
THAT WENT BETTER THAN EXPECTED
SPUT
FLUTTER
`CEPT FOR PERCH

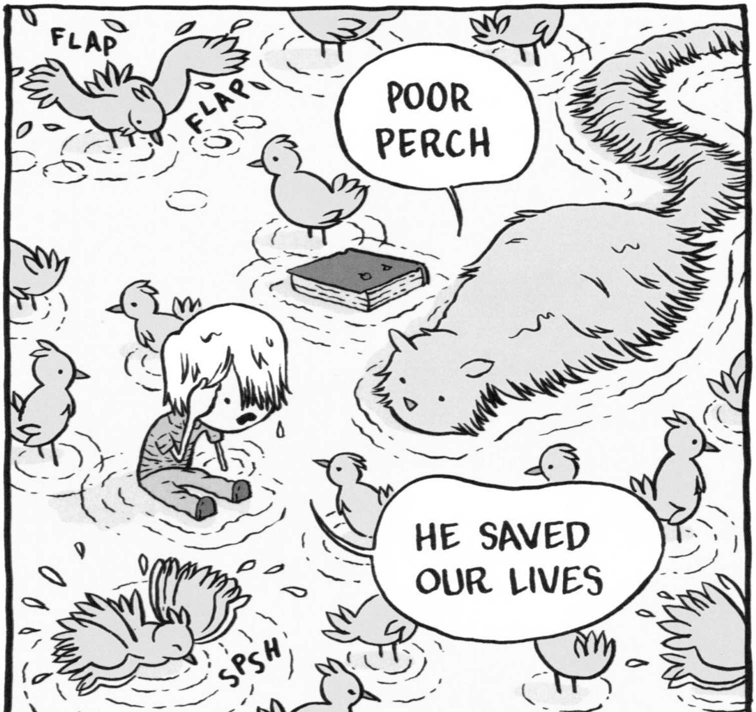
FLAP
FLAP
POOR PERCH
HE SAVED OUR LIVES
SPSH

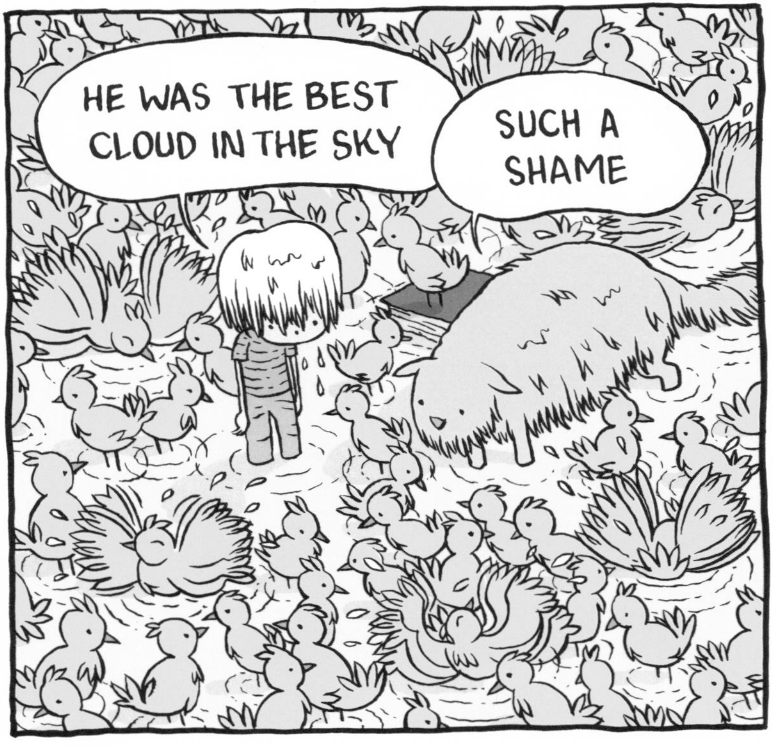
HE WAS THE BEST CLOUD IN THE SKY
SUCH A SHAME

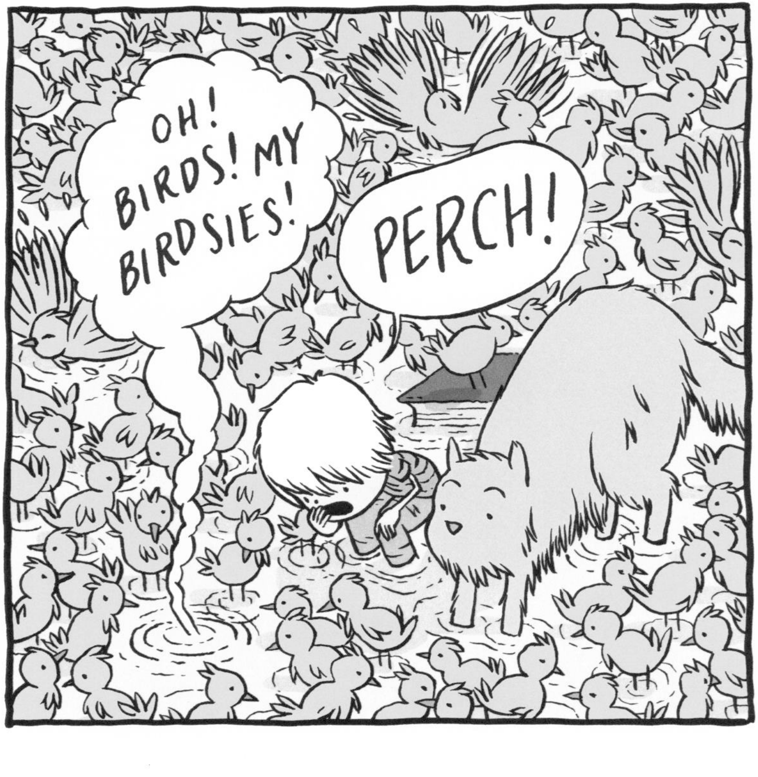
OH! BIRDS! MY BIRDSIES!
PERCH!

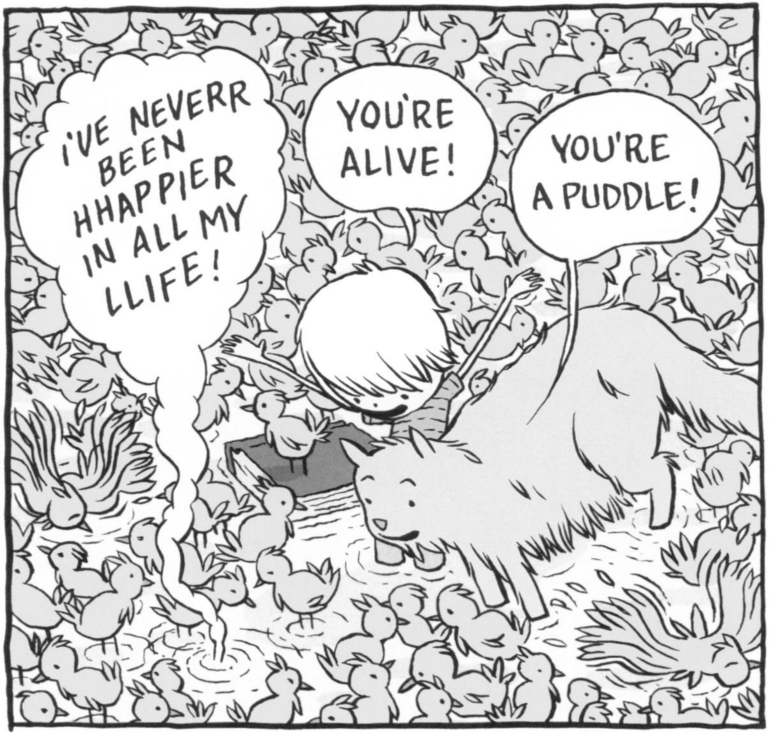
I'VE NEVERR BEEN HHAPPIER IN ALL MY LLIFE!
YOU'RE ALIVE!
YOU'RE A PUDDLE!

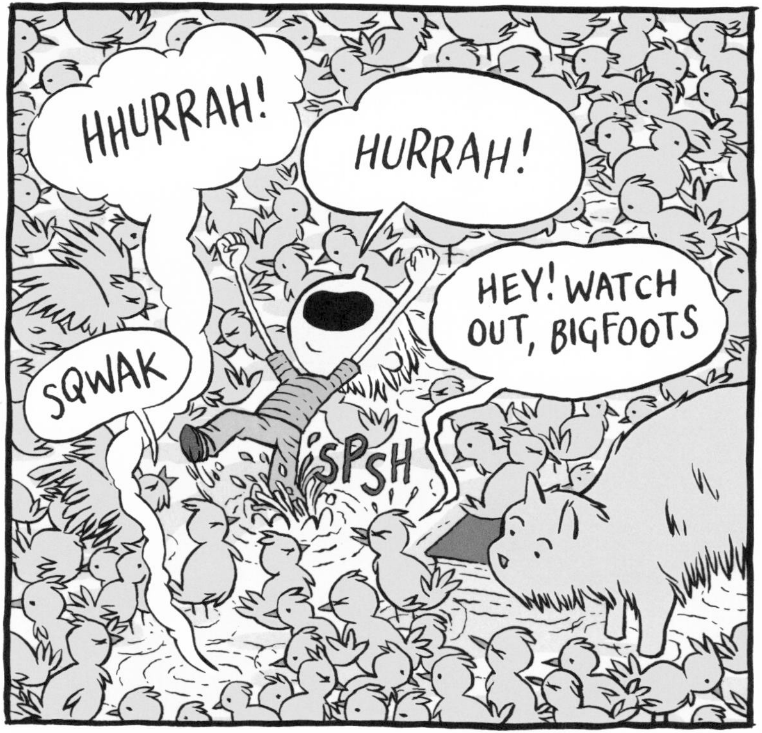
HHURRAH!
HURRAH!
HEY! WATCH OUT, BIGFOOTS
SQWAK
SPSH

WHY, IT'S THAT KID AND HIS DOG!
HE'S NOT A DOG!
CAREFUL! THEY ARE SAVAGES
SQWAK
Y'JERKS
SKUAWK

NNOW BEE NICE
LET HIM ALONE!
LET'S PECK THEIR FACES
THAT ONE TRIED TO EAT ME!
SQUAWK
WRETCHES
LOUSY

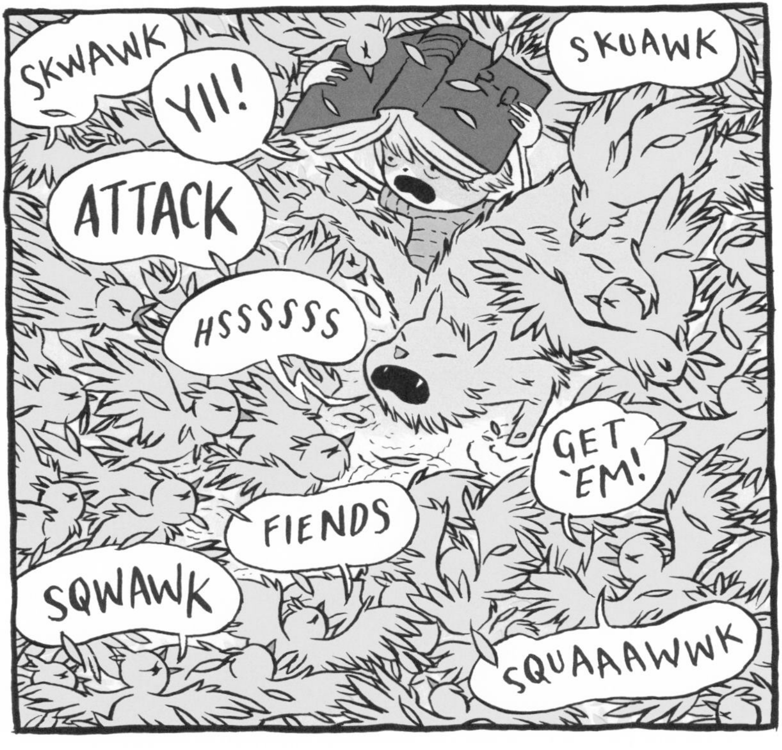
SKWAWK
YII!
SKUAWK
ATTACK
HSSSSSS
GET 'EM!
FIENDS
SQWAWK
SQUAAAWWK

SKWAHK
HALT
QUIT IT!
RETREAT IS USELESS
HISSSS
BIRDS SHALL PREVAIL!

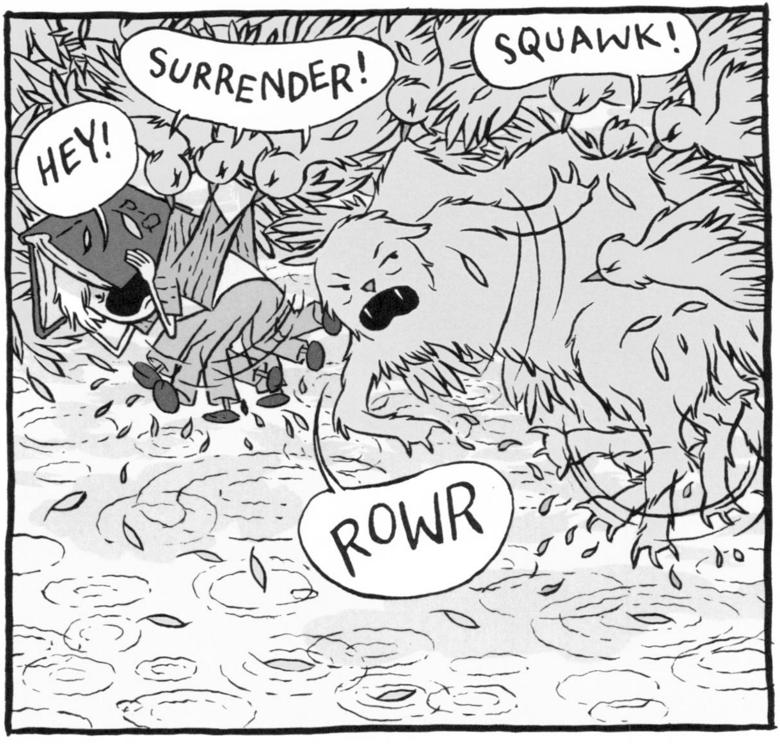
HEY!
SURRENDER!
SQUAWK!
ROWR

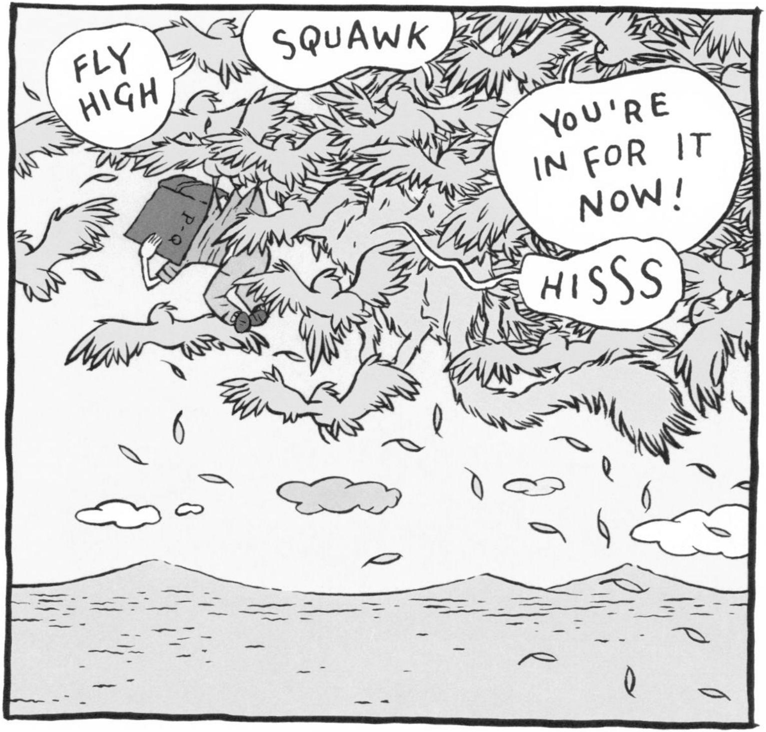
FLY HIGH
SQUAWK
YOU'RE IN FOR IT NOW!
HISSS

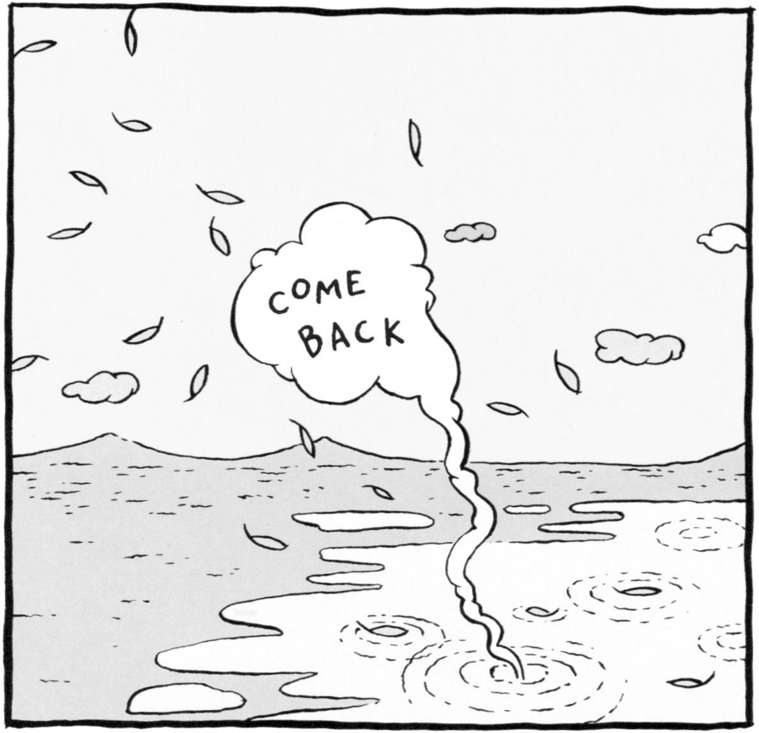
COME BACK

WHERE SHOULD WE DROP 'EM?
THE BOG OF BONES
THE CHASM AT POINT PUTRID

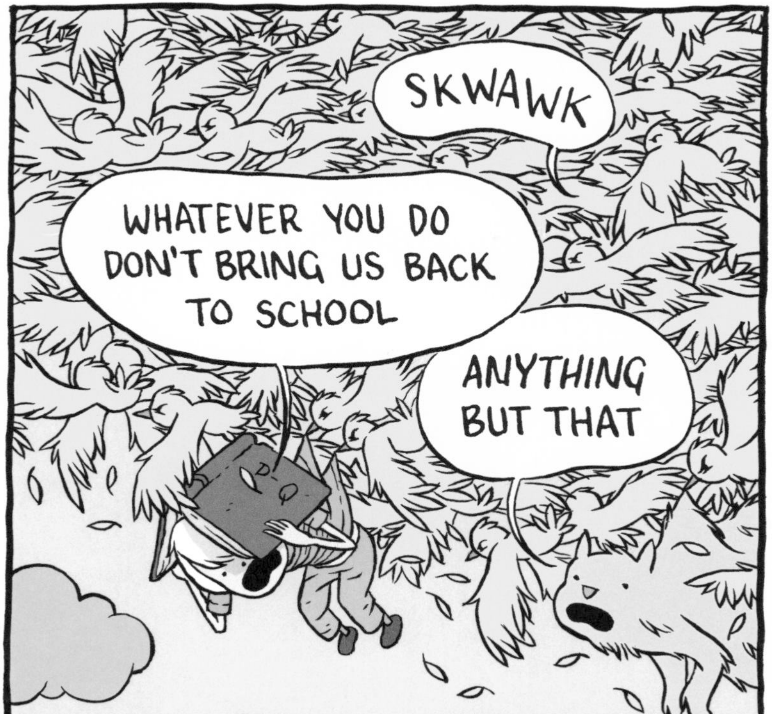
SKWAWK
WHATEVER YOU DO DON'T BRING US BACK TO SCHOOL
ANYTHING BUT THAT

SCHOOL, HM? WHICH ONE?
TELLUS!
DENKER AVENUE ELEMENTARY
ROOM 22

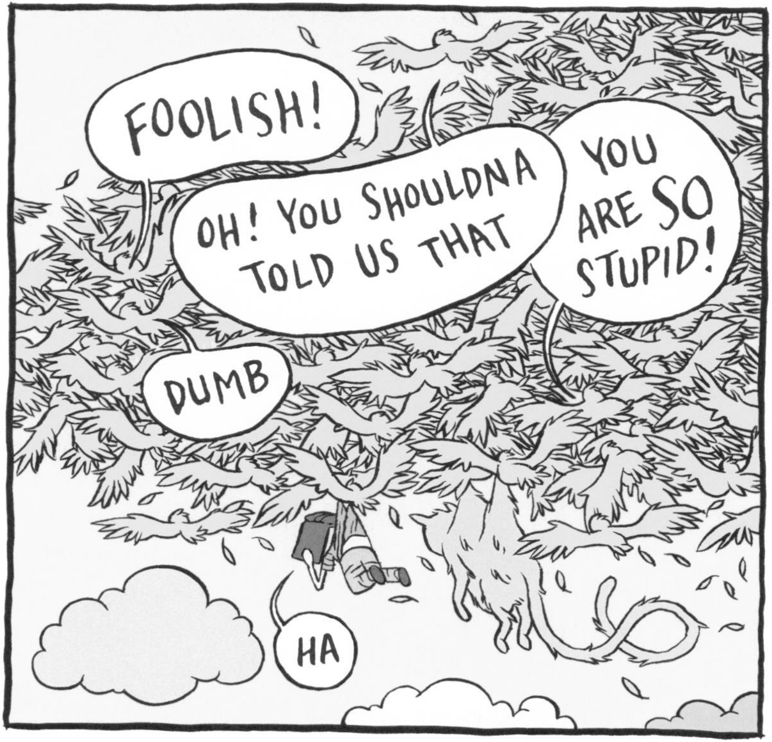
FOOLISH!
OH! YOU SHOULDNA TOLD US THAT
YOU ARE SO STUPID!
DUMB
HA

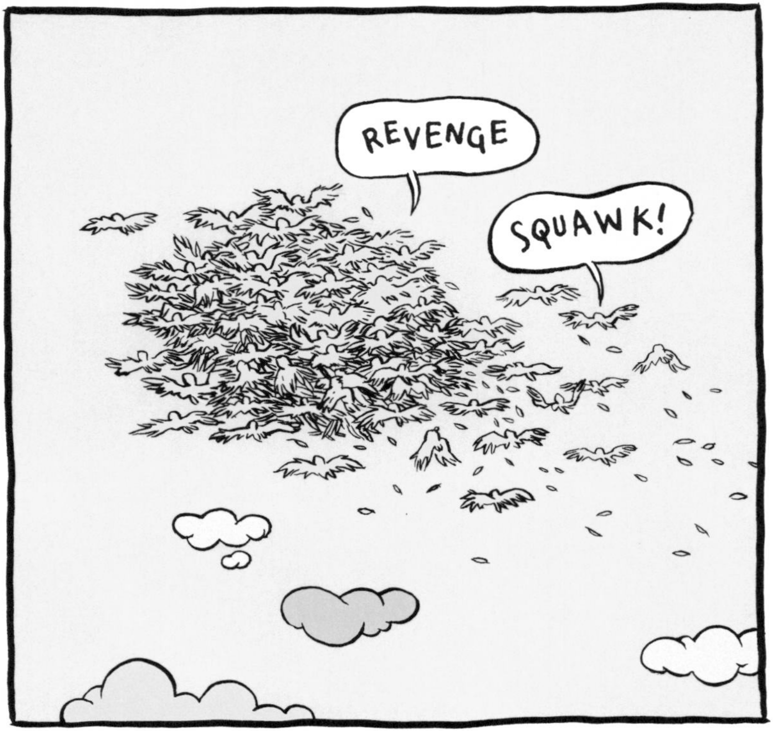
REVENGE
SQUAWK!

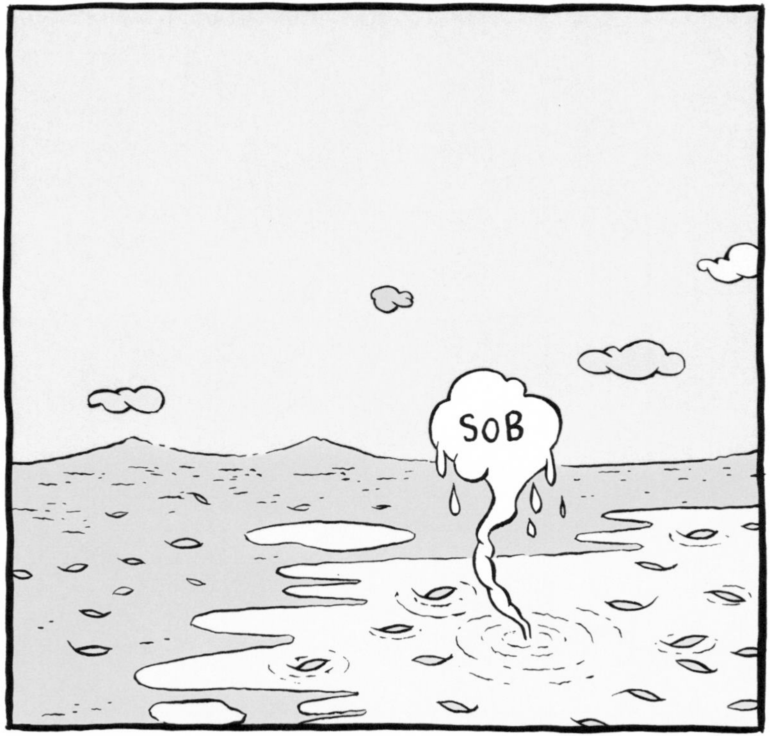
SOB

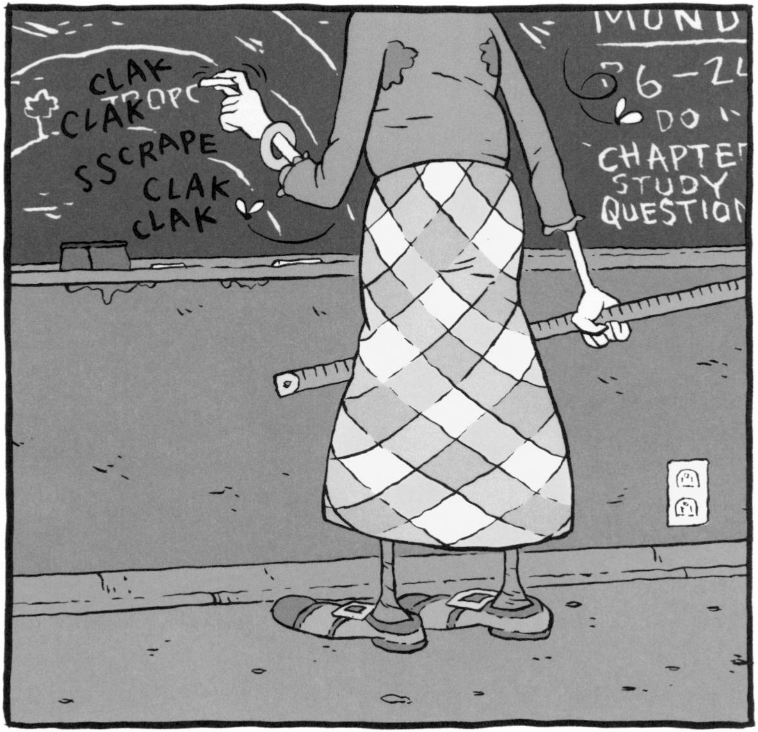
CLAK
CLAK
SSCRAPE
CLAK
CLAK
DO
CHAPTE
STUDY
QUESTIO

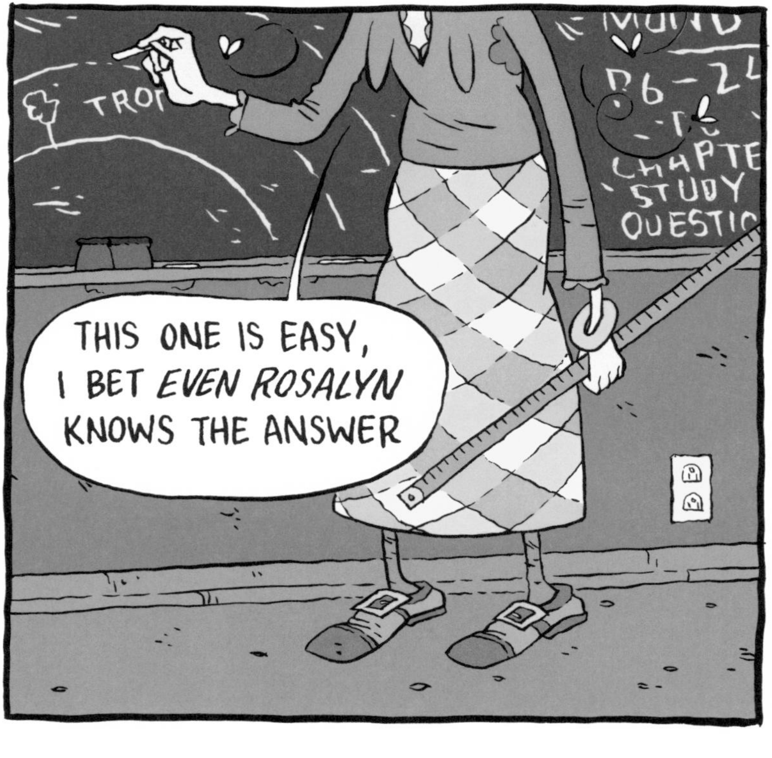
THIS ONE IS EASY,
I BET *EVEN ROSALYN*
KNOWS THE ANSWER

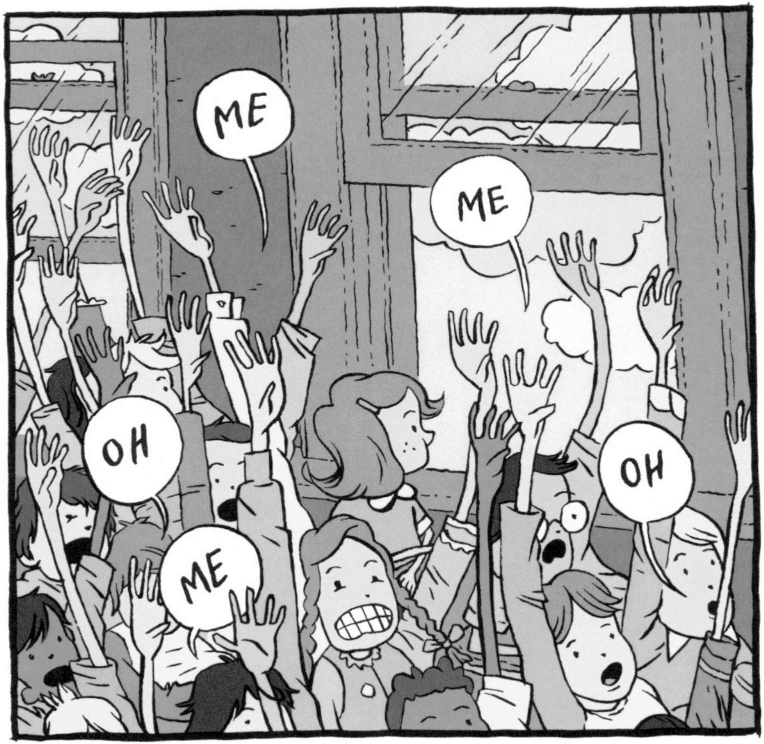
ME
ME
OH
OH
ME

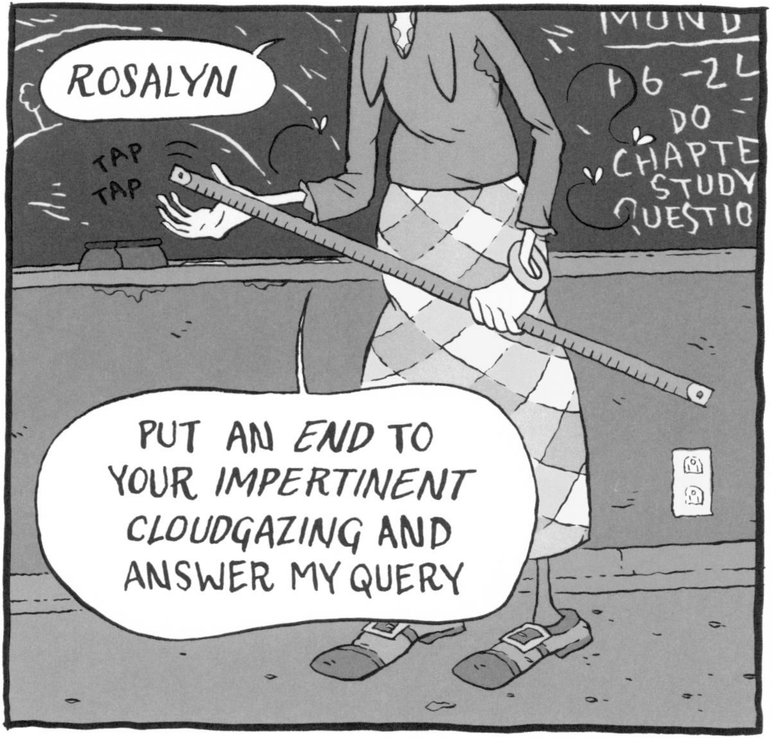
ROSALYN
TAP TAP
DO CHAPTE STUDY QUESTIO
PUT AN *END* TO YOUR *IMPERTINENT* CLOUDGAZING AND ANSWER MY QUERY

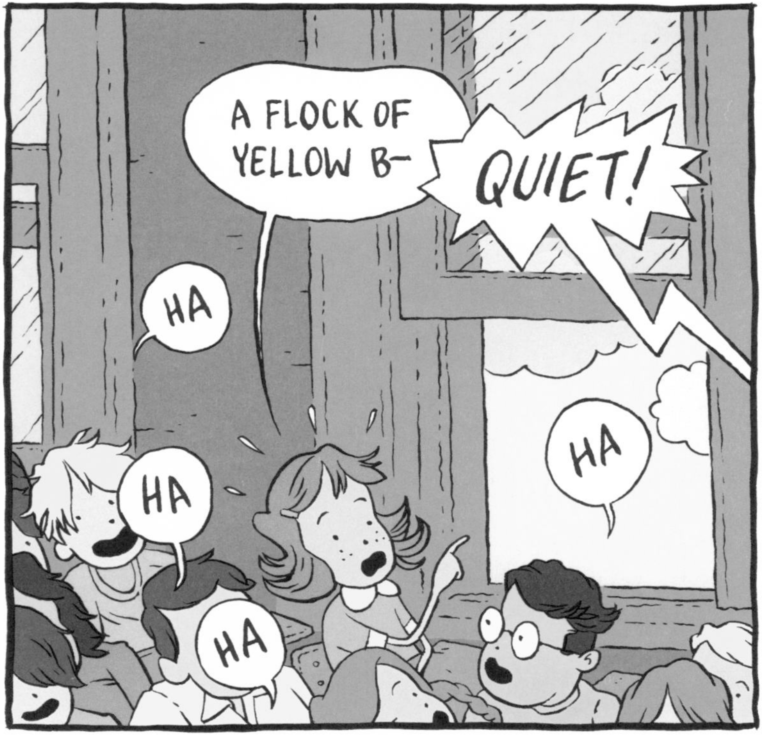
A FLOCK OF
YELLOW B–
QUIET!
HA
HA
HA
HA

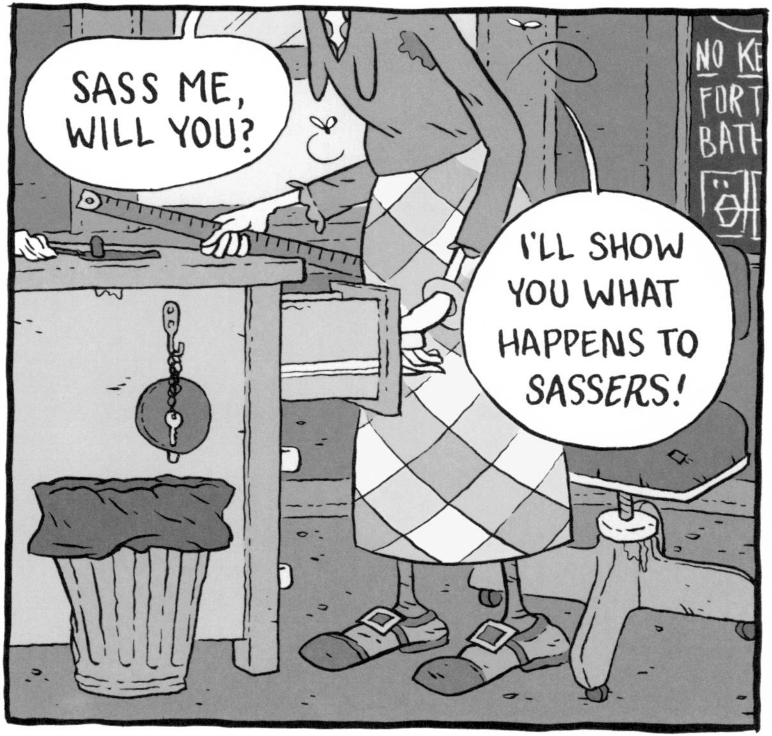
SASS ME, WILL YOU?
I'LL SHOW YOU WHAT HAPPENS TO SASSERS!

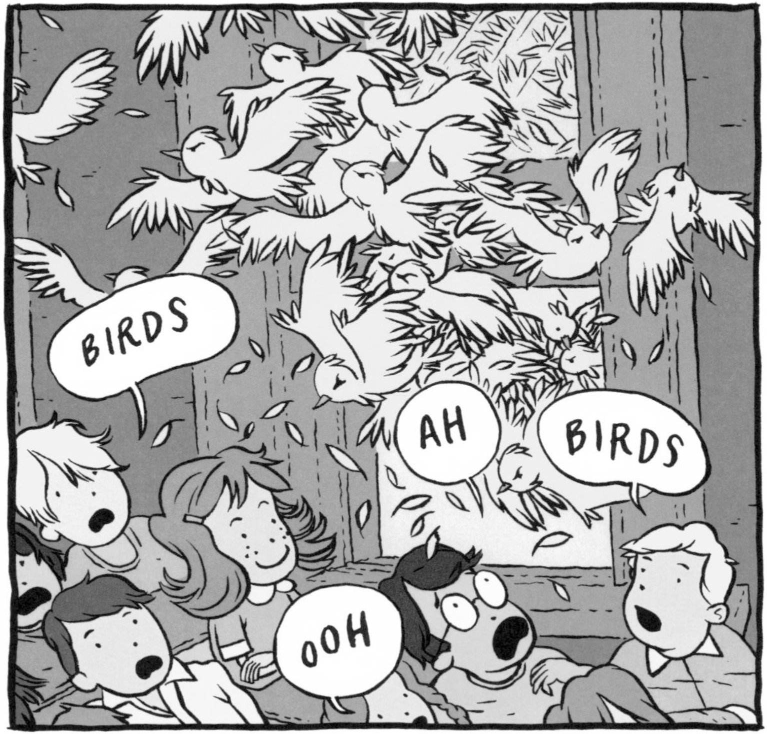
BIRDS
AH
BIRDS
OOH

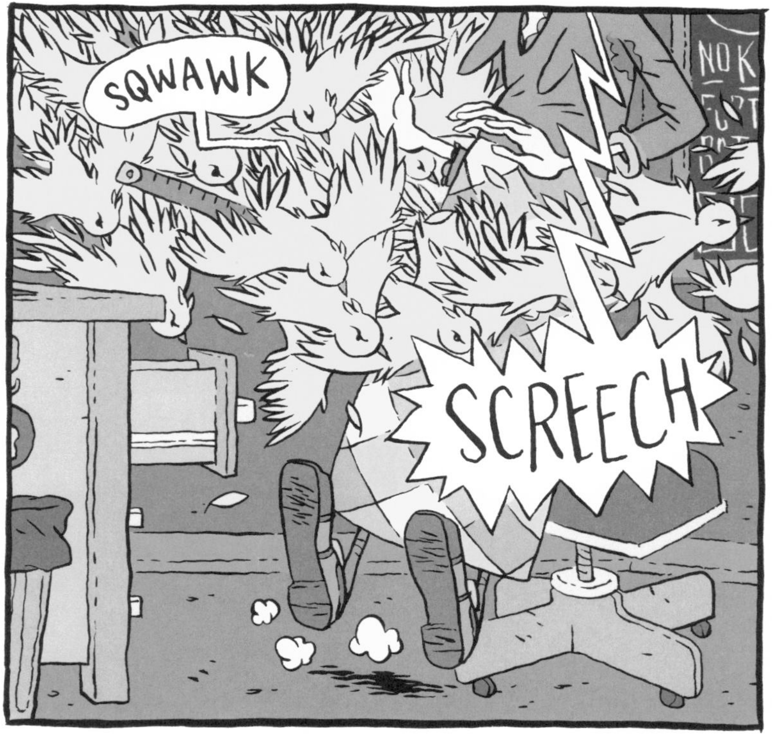
SQWAWK
SCREECH

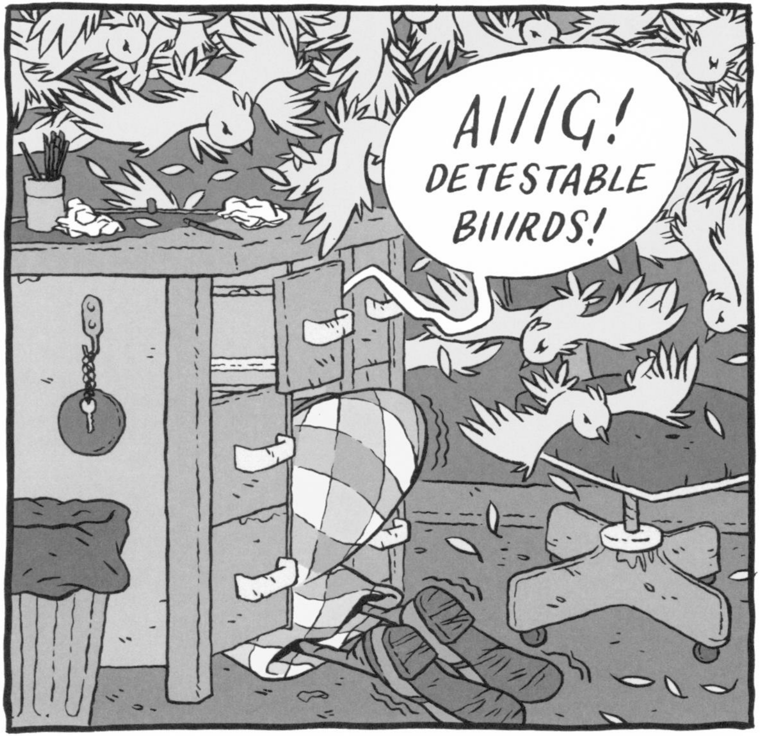
AIIIG!
DETESTABLE
BIIIRDS!

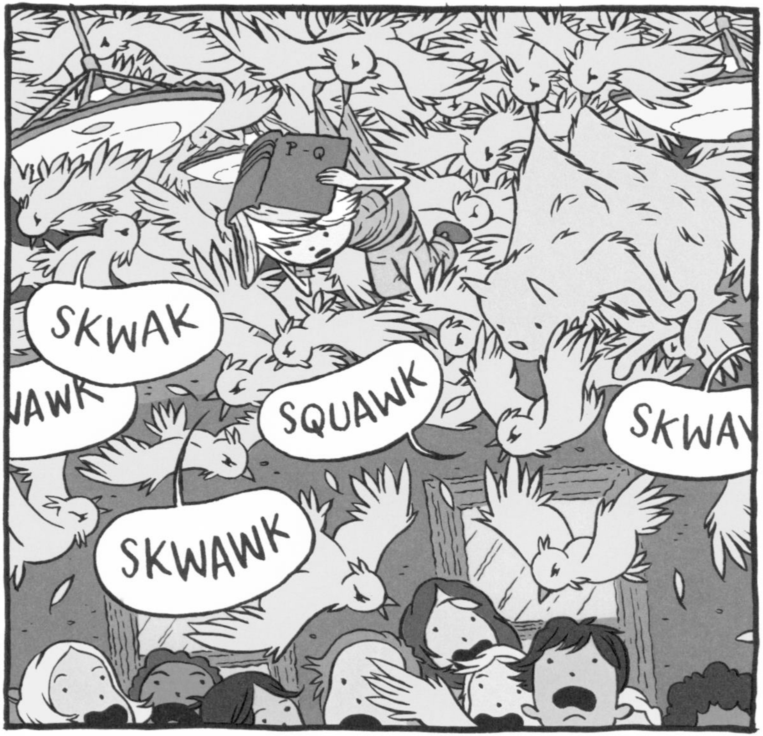
P-Q
SKWAK
AWK
SQUAWK
SKWA
SKWAWK

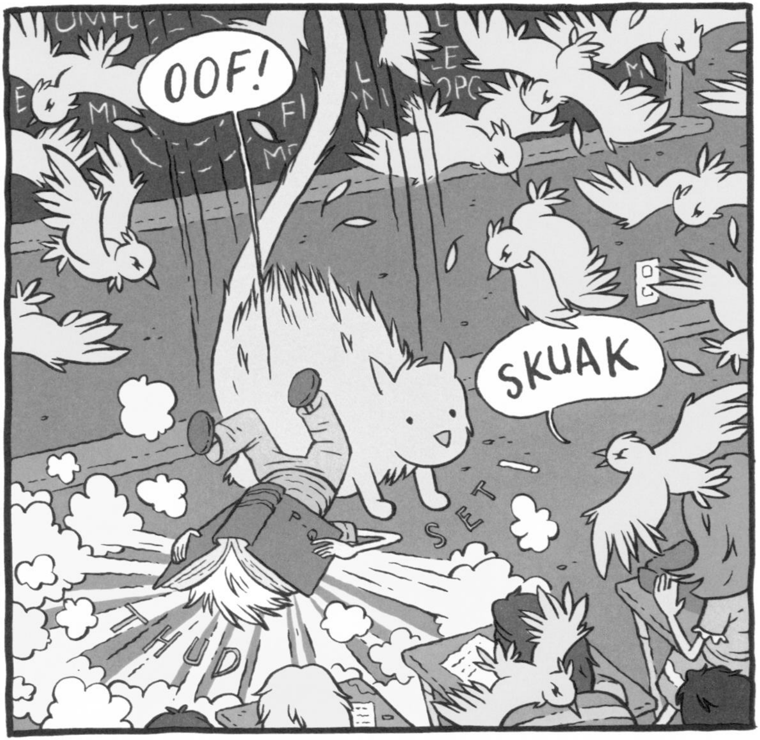
OOF!
SKUAK
THUD

SKWAWK
SQUAWK
THAT'LL TEACH HIM
SQU
SKWAWK
SKWAWK
VICTORY IS OURS

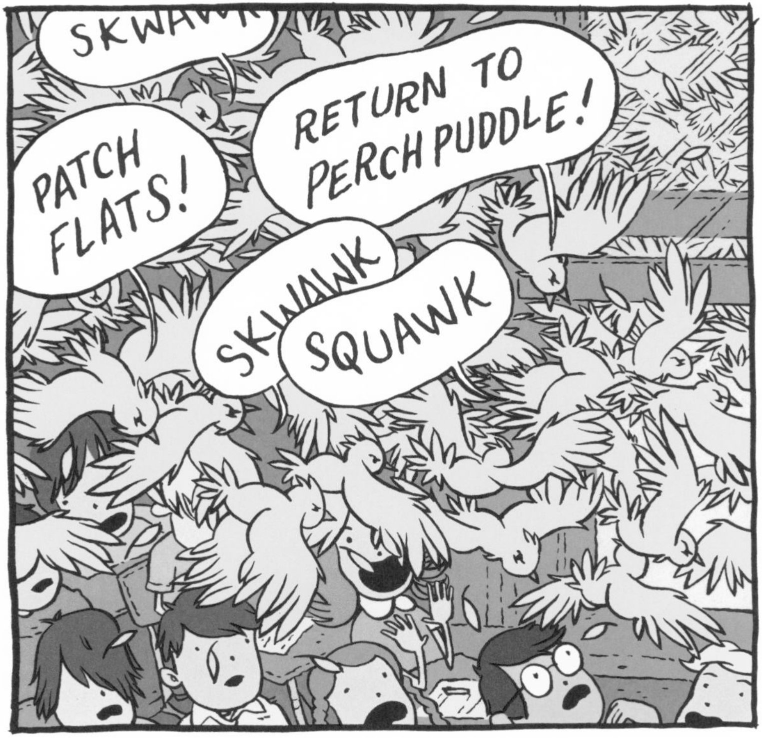
SKWAW
PATCH FLATS!
RETURN TO PERCH PUDDLE!
SKWAWK
SQUAWK

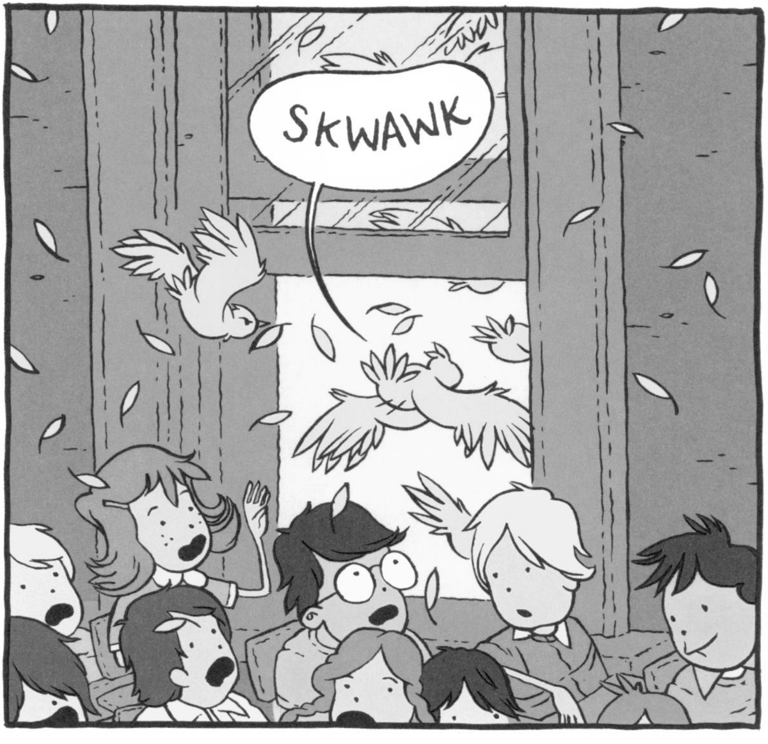
SKWAWK

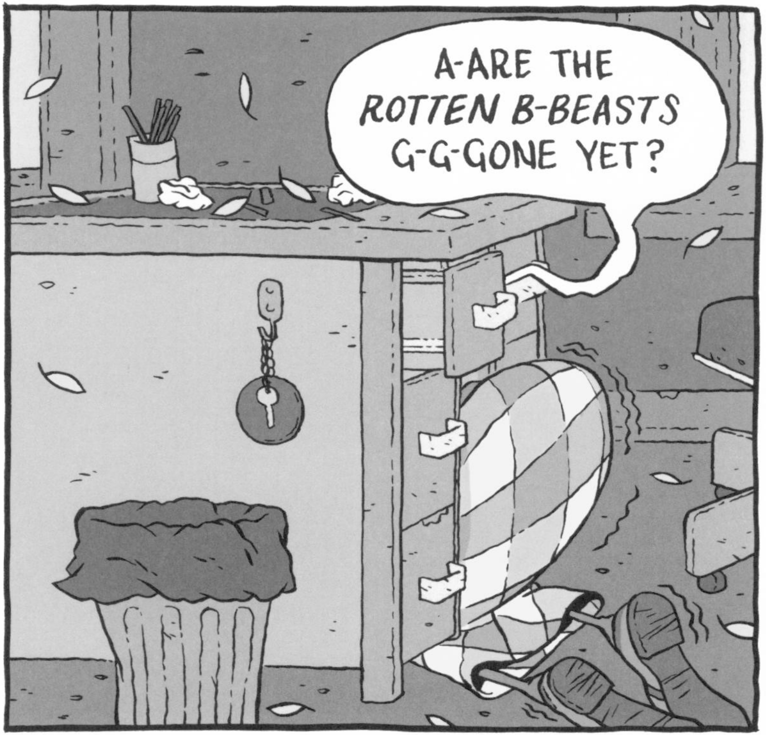
A-ARE THE *ROTTEN B-BEASTS* G-G-GONE YET?

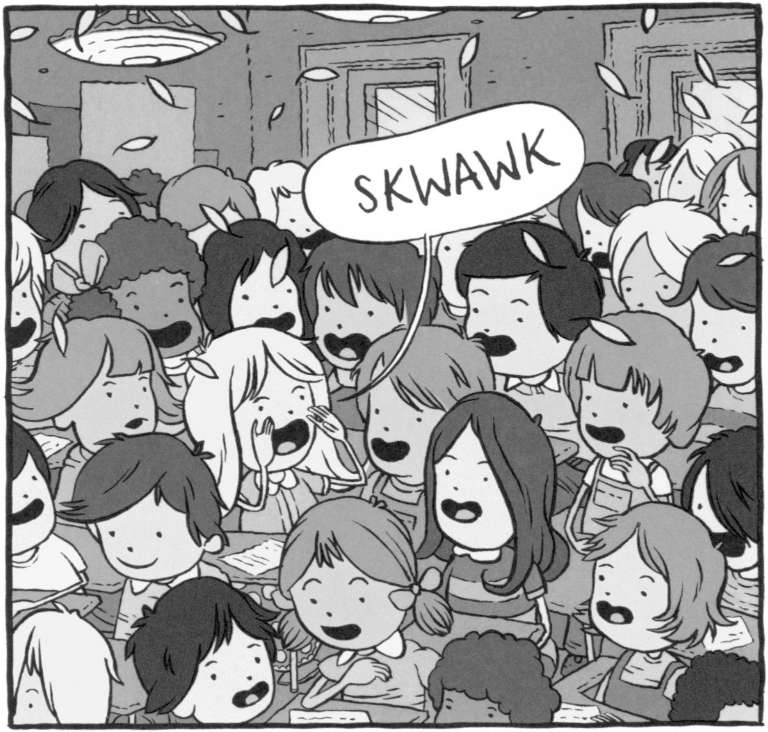
SKWAWK

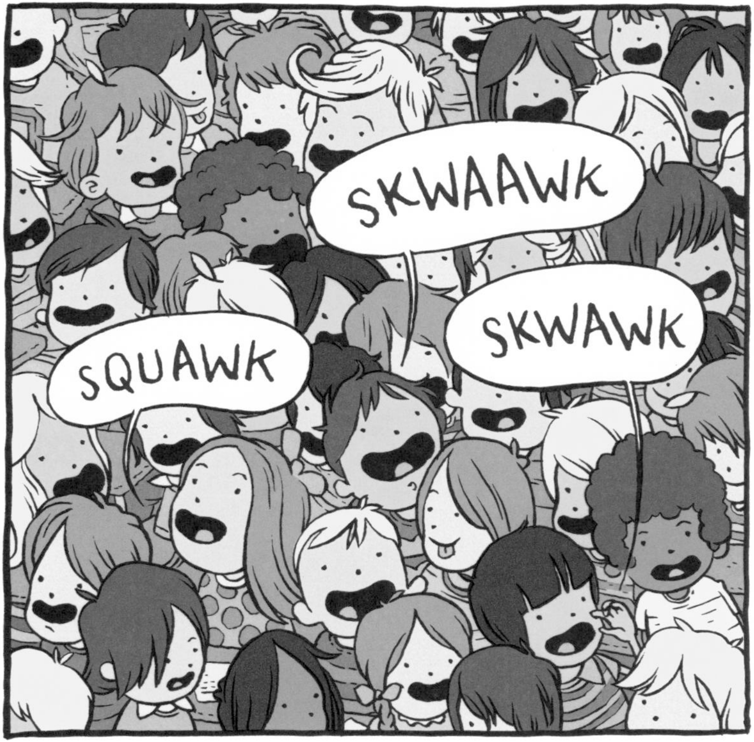
SKWAAAWK
SQUAWK
SKWAWK

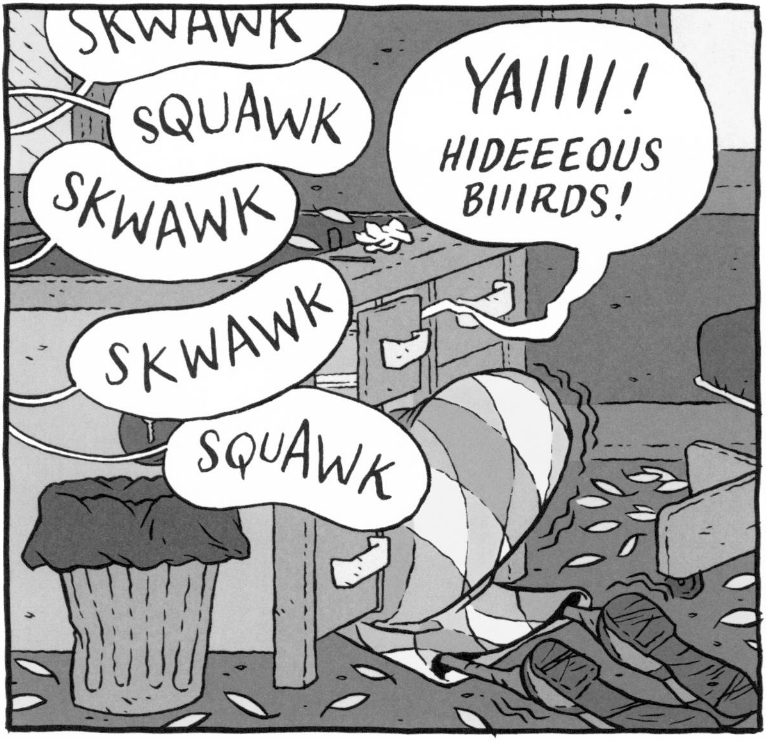
SKWAWK
SQUAWK
SKWAWK
SKWAWK
SQUAWK
YAIIII! HIDEEEOUS BIIIRDS!

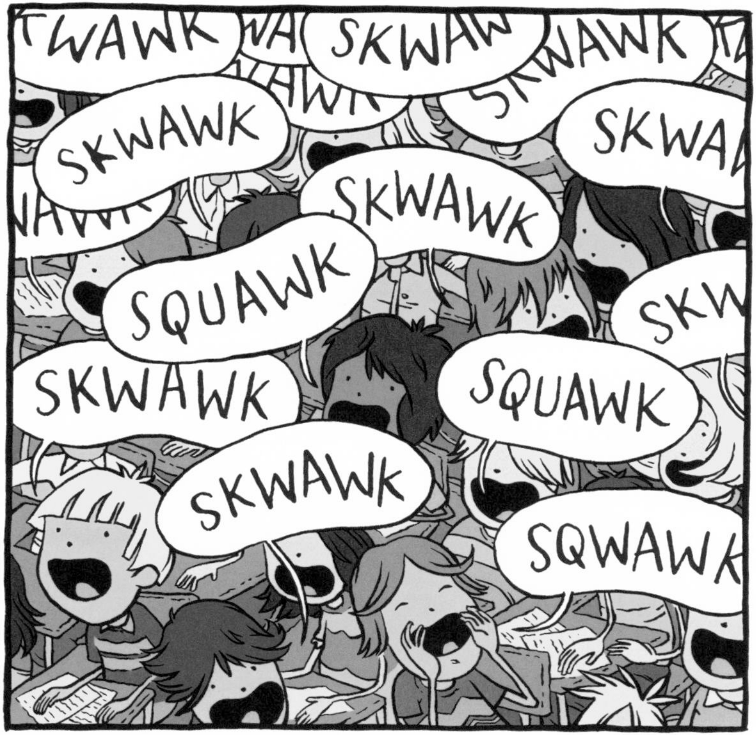

TWAWK
SKWAW
SKWAWK
SKWAWK
SKWA
SKWAWK
SQUAWK
SKW
SKWAWK
SQUAWK
SKWAWK
SQWAWK

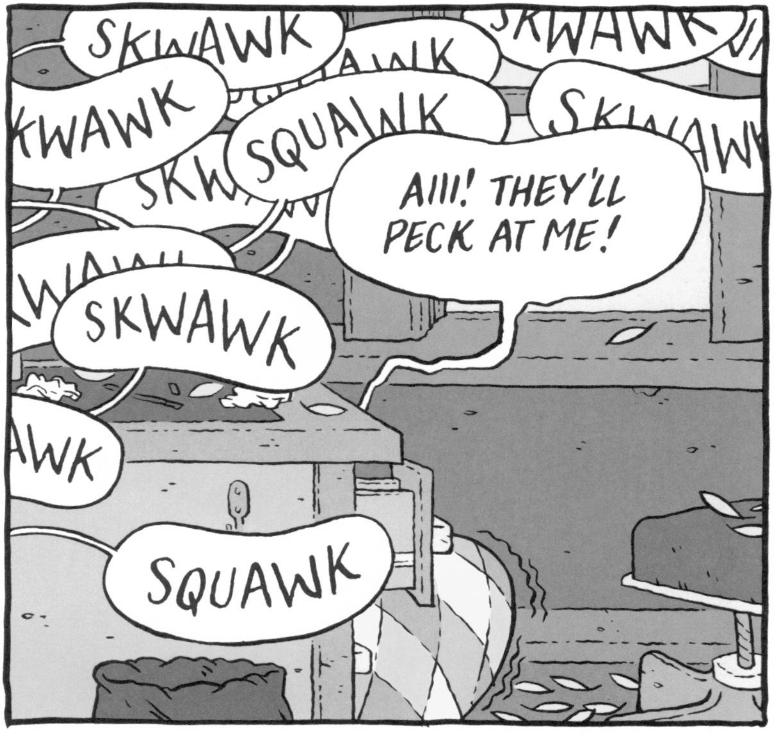
SKWAWK
KWAWK
AIII! THEY'LL PECK AT ME!
SKWAWK
AWK
SQUAWK

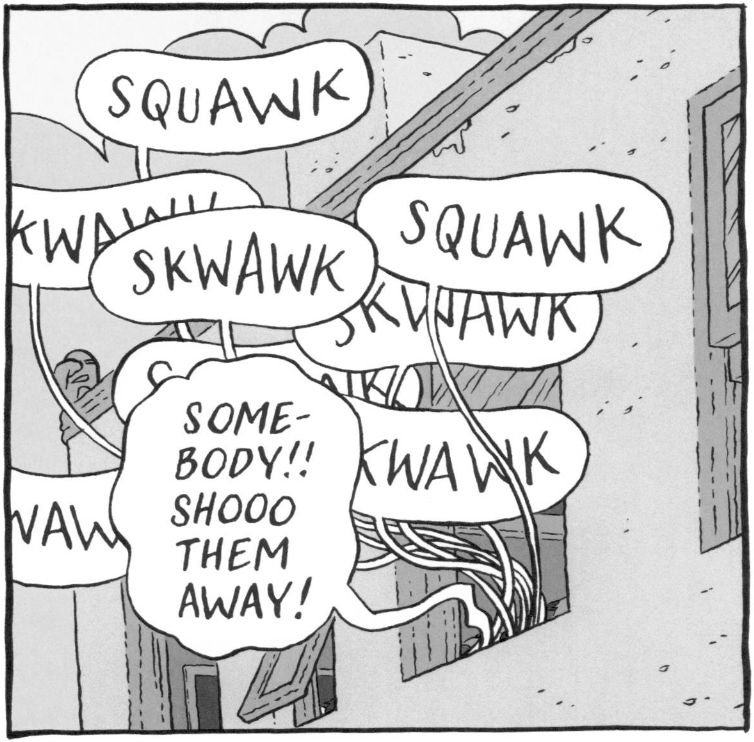
SQUAWK
SKWAWK
SQUAWK
SOME-BODY!! SHOOO THEM AWAY!

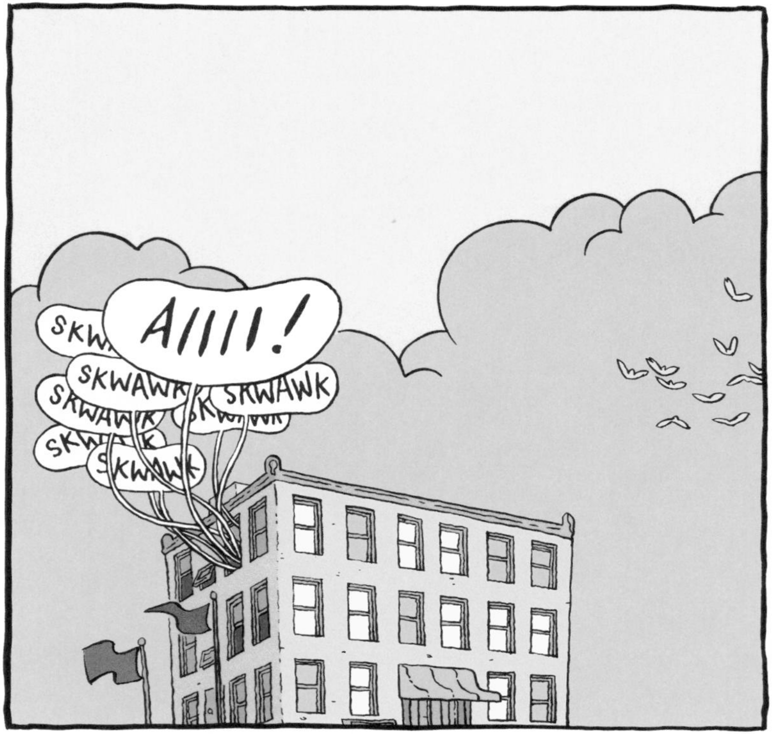
AIIII!
SKWAWK
SKWAWK

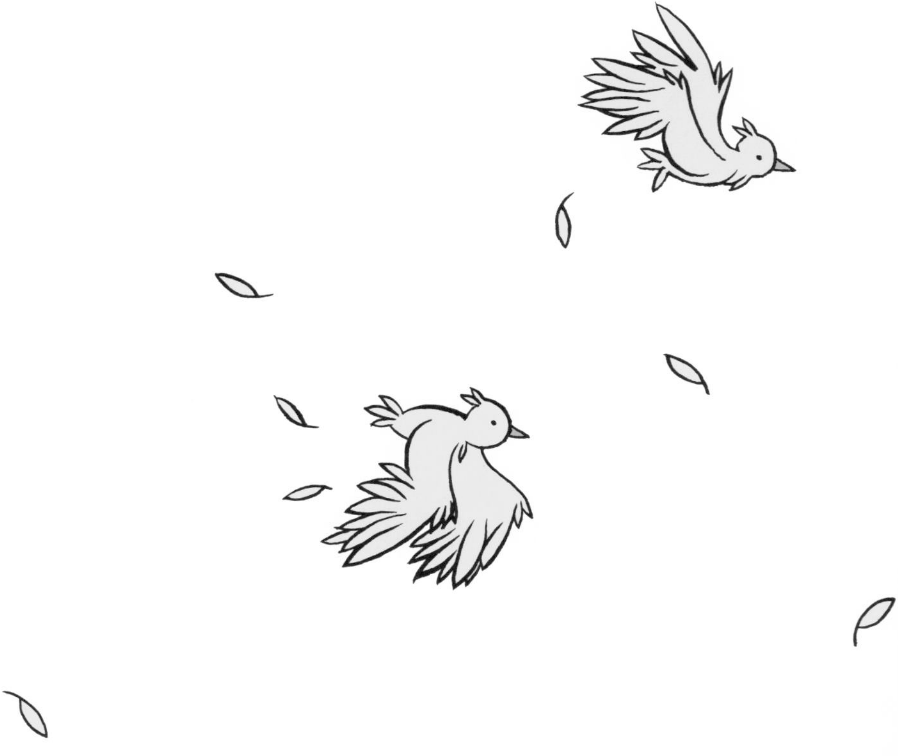

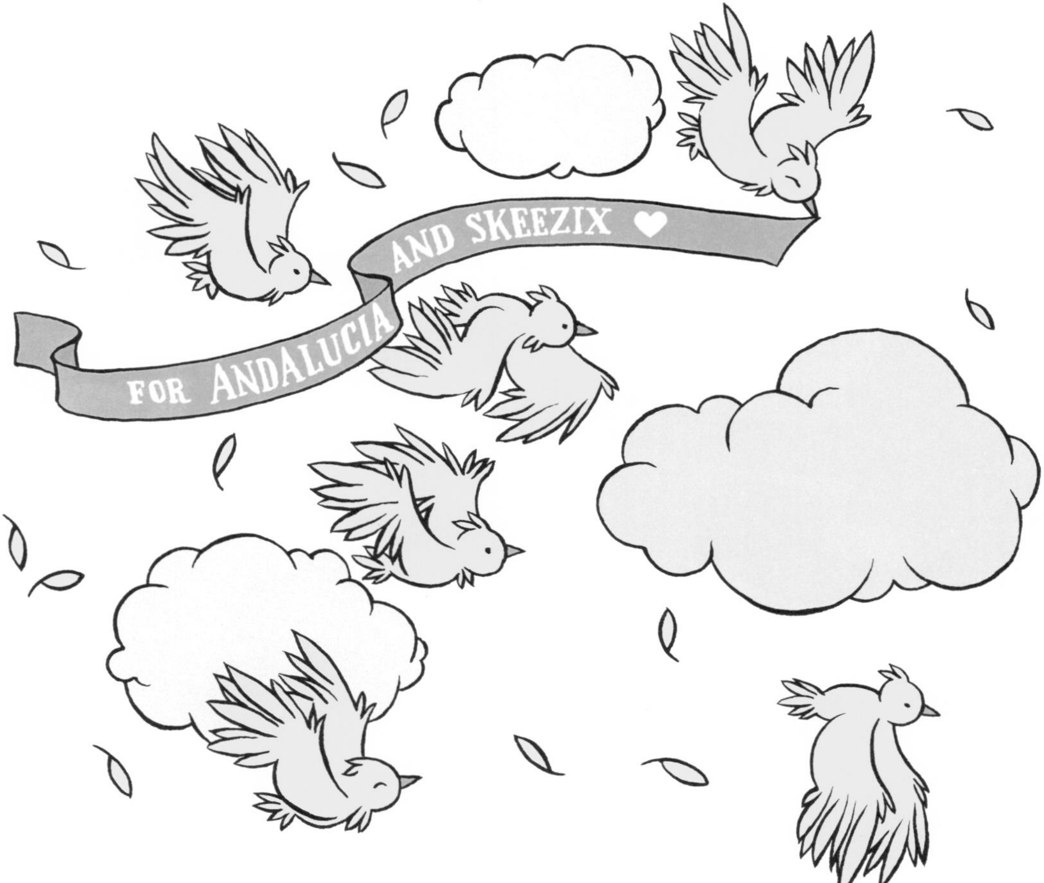
FOR ANDALUCIA AND SKEEZIX ♥

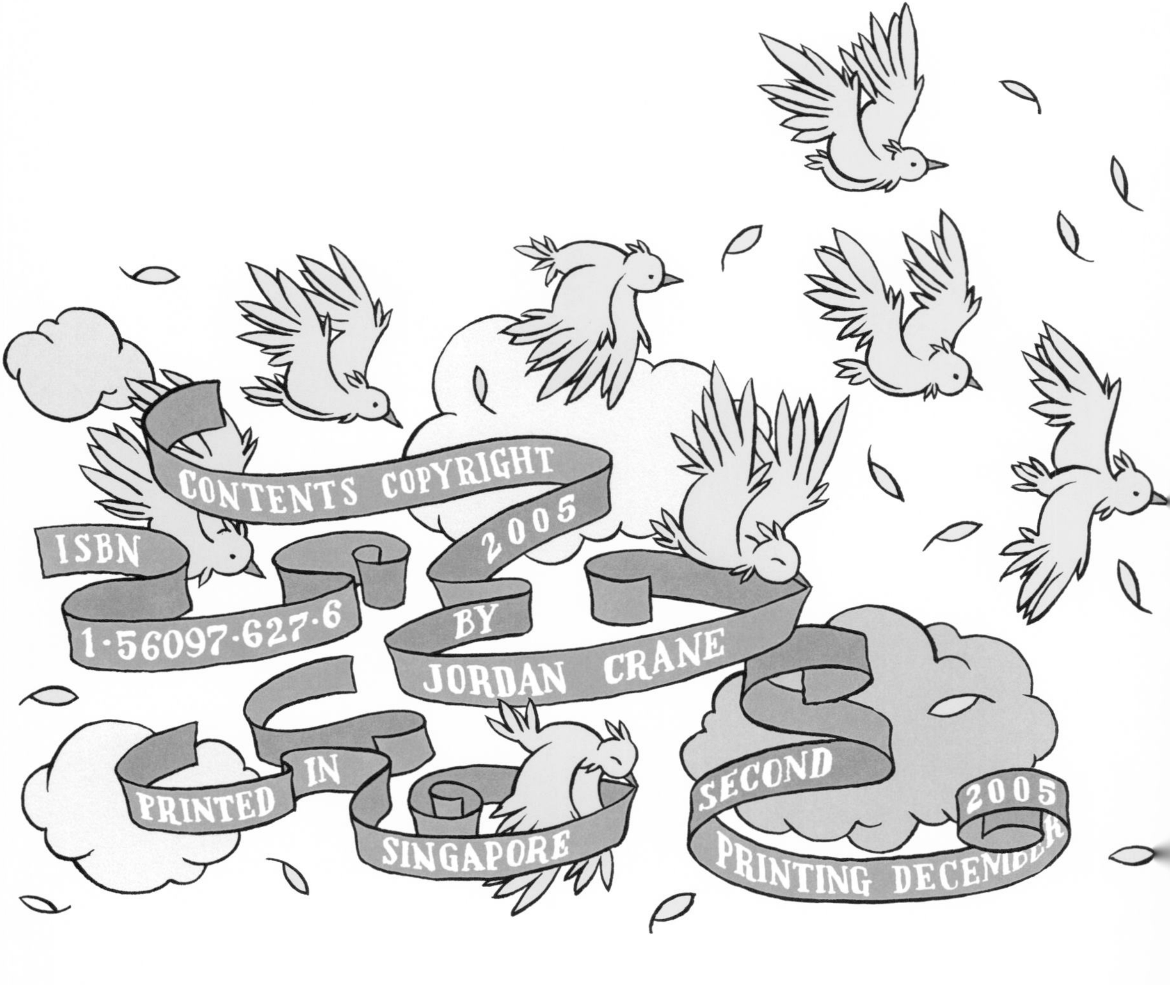

CONTENTS COPYRIGHT 2005
BY
JORDAN CRANE
ISBN
1-56097-627-6
PRINTED IN
SINGAPORE
SECOND
PRINTING DECEMBER
2005

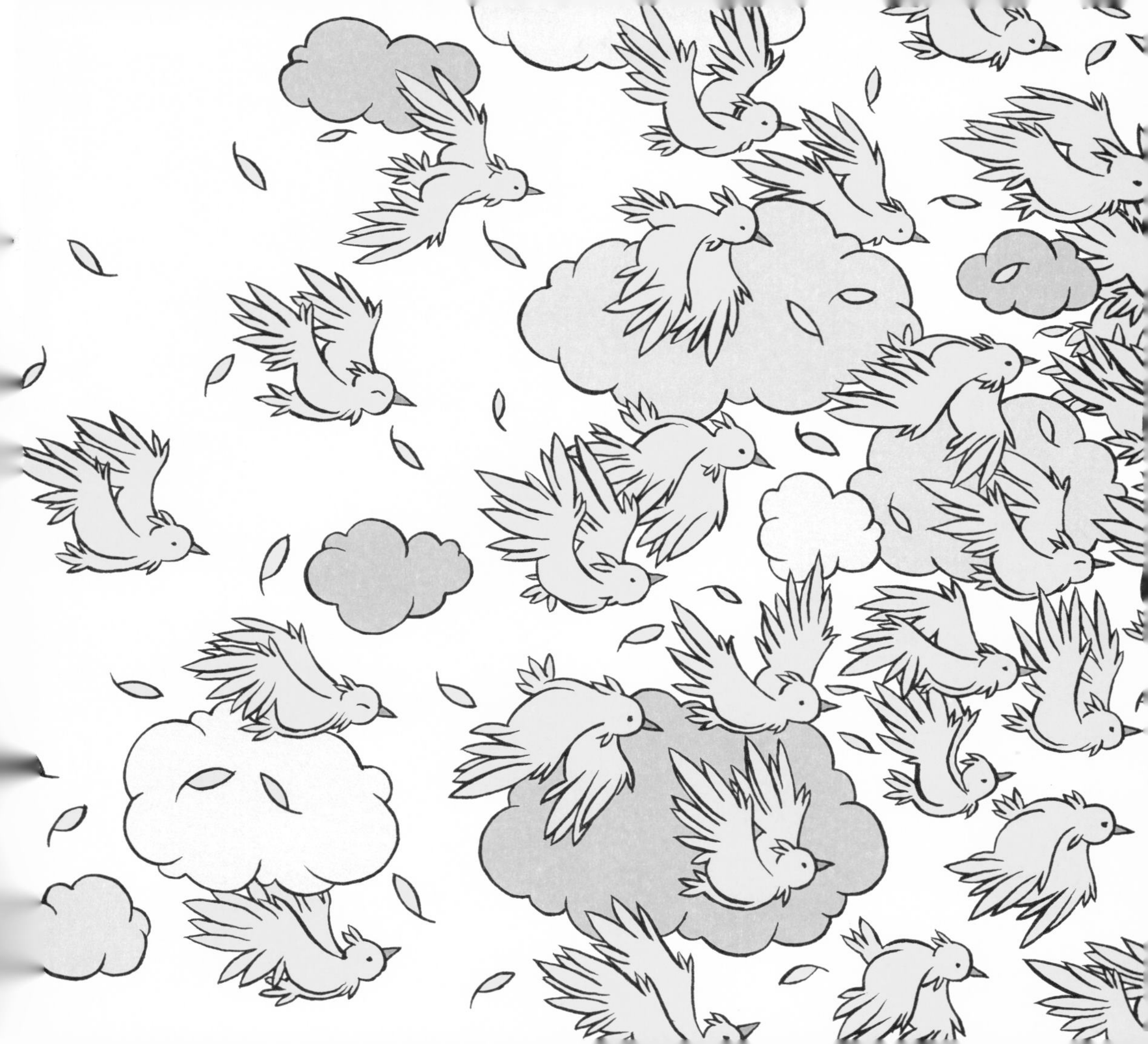

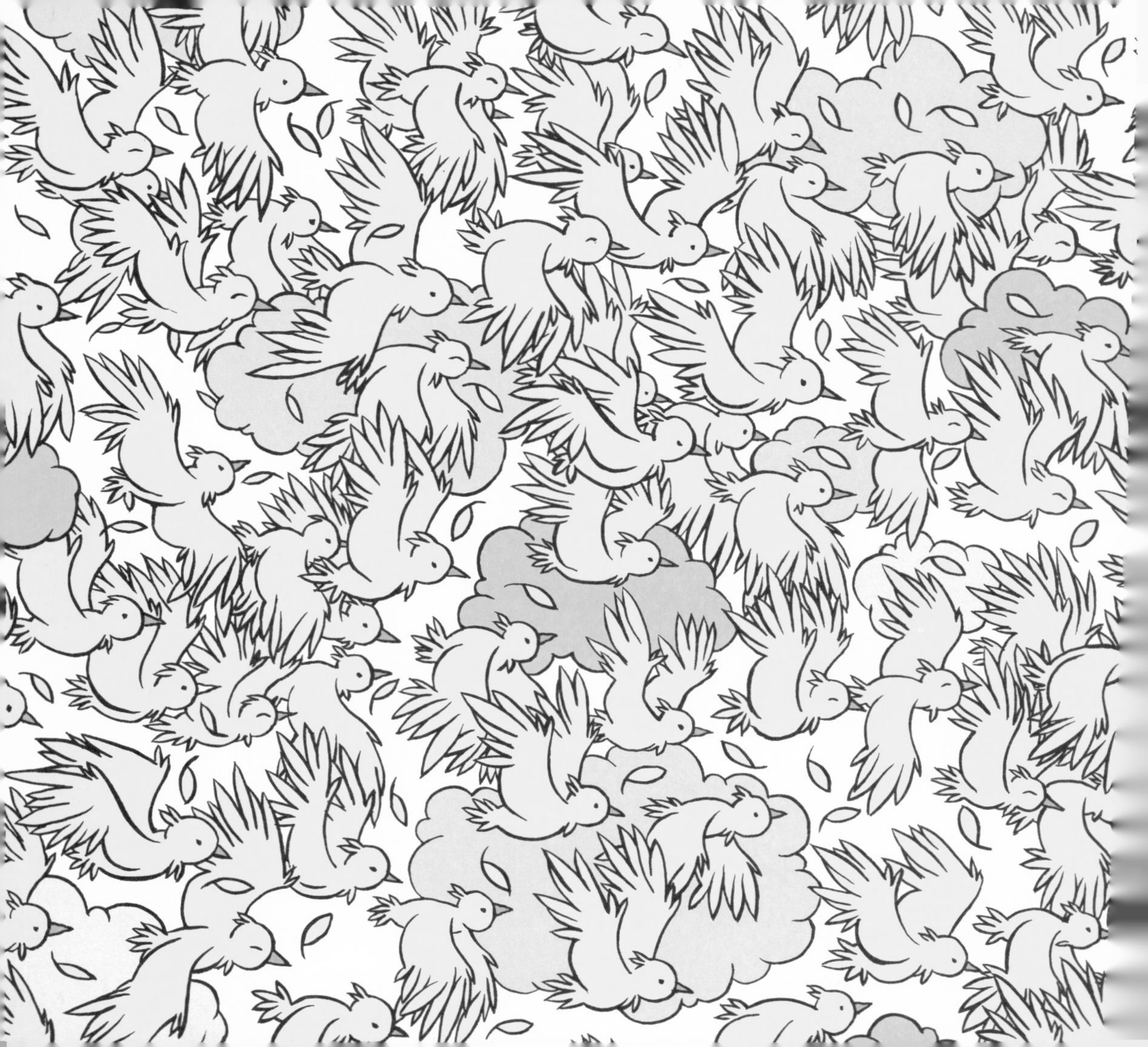